Skipton High Street, 1830. Victorian woodcut

SKIPTON AND THE
CRAVEN DALES

Skipton Castle Gateway, with its sturdy drum towers, has been a symbol of Skipton since the early part of the 17th century. It was the creation of Henry, 5th Earl of Cumberland (1591-1643), who was especially fond of architecture. Lady Anne Clifford (1589-1675), who restored the Castle after its 'slighting' during the Commonwealth, had the Clifford motto – 'Des Or Mais', meaning Henceforth – set in stone on the top of the outer gatehouse walls. Skipton Building Society, the largest employer in the town, adopted the outline of the Castle gateway as its emblem.

SKIPTON AND THE CRAVEN DALES

W. R. Mitchell

Phillimore

2006

Published by
PHILLIMORE & CO. LTD
Shopwyke Manor Barn, Chichester, West Sussex, England
www.phillimore.co.uk

ISBN   1-86077-390-7
ISBN 13   978-1-86077-390-7

Printed and bound in Great Britain by
THE CROMWELL PRESS LTD
Trowbridge, Wiltshire

For
Arthur Raistrick

Contents

List of Illustrations

Frontispiece: Skipton Castle Gateway.

Acknowledgements

I was christened in Holy Trinity Church at Skipton in January 1928, and spent the first twenty years of my life in the town. As a child, I was taken for a walk 'up the Bailey', in the shadow of the gaunt walls of a castle occupied by the Cliffords, who were for centuries the resident aristocracy. At school, with Harry Gill as a history teacher, I absorbed the lore and legends of the Craven district, of which Skipton was the undisputed capital.

In those inter-war years, Skipton was conspicuously a textile town, and friends and neighbours could recount tales of life 'at t'mill'. A forest of lanky chimneys breathed smoke into the thin air or, if there were a sudden downdraught, blotted out the streets. A thousand looms clattered. The air around a weaving shed held the sweet smell of damp cotton. Dewhurst's, the largest mill, had a brick chimney so tall it had the visual emphasis of an exclamation mark. A steam whistle regulated the working day, and hundreds of textile workers scurrying along the Broughton Road at teatime moved cheek by jowl with livestock being driven from the adjacent auction mart.

Serving my time as a journalist on the *Craven Herald & Pioneer*, I toured the district, initially on foot or by bus, and met informative folk such as Sam Stables of Grassington and Tot Lord, who at Settle mixed greengrocery with archaeology. P.P. Illingworth, the living history book, knew the names of virtually everyone in town, as well as their initials. He regaled me with local folk tales when, attending the funeral of the author C.J. Cutcliffe Hyne, we strode along a dusty road through the glacial trough of Upper Wharfedale from Grassington to Kettlewell.

On Monday evenings, sitting on hard wood in a steeply banked lecture hall of the Science and Art School with members of the Craven Naturalists' and Scientific Association, I absorbed yet more information about the locality as hand-tinted slides were projected onto a huge screen. At Giggleswick, Leta Douglas introduced me to the folk dances of the Craven Dales she had tirelessly researched. I chatted with Geoffrey Rowley, a local solicitor who was studying human affairs at Skipton with an enthusiasm not known since W.H. Dawson had written the standard history of the town in 1882. The Craven Museum has been a constant inspiration.

Harry J. Scott, founder of *The Dalesman*, who worked as a sub-editor at the *Herald* during the Second World War, invited me to join him and thus began over forty years of hard but enjoyable editorial work at Clapham, a village overshadowed by

Ingleborough. Harry quietly insisted that we put people before things so I interviewed hundreds of people. On visits to the Raistricks, Arthur and his wife Elizabeth, who lived in a converted barn at Linton-in-Craven, I sampled Elizabeth's freshly made scones and was then updated by Arthur on his latest research. George Gill, the owner of Stump Cross Cave, near Craven Cross on breezy Greenhow, related tales of the lead miners and roused for my delectation some of the ghosts of the area. Cyril Harrington, a former art master at Giggleswick School, had a fresh way of considering old topics. In a *Dalesman* article about Skipton, he assessed market day as a time 'when the din and clatter, bustle and hum make up a movement allegro in the great pastoral symphony of the Dales.'

Sebastian Fattorini, of Skipton Castle, introduced me to his collection of uncommon prints which has been owned by his family for over half a century. At Skipton Library I accessed the Rowley collection of old photographs, a selection of which appears in this book by courtesy of Mrs V. Rowley. Stamper Metcalfe – his Christian name being the surname of a family linked by marriage – arrived at my home unexpectedly with photographs of Old Giggleswick I had not seen before. Christine Denmead drew the map of Skipton and that part of Craven covered by this book.

Illustrations from the following sources are cordially acknowledged: A. Wulstan Atkins, 135; Dan Binns (courtesy of David Binns), 3, 24, 25; W.H. Dawson (*History of Skipton*, 1882), 10, 12, 13, 14; Derek Soames, 87, 88; David Hoyle, 34; Edward Jeffrey, 2, 19, 47, 145, 146; Giggleswick Church, 114; E.H. Horner, 38, 118; Stamper Metcalfe, 126-7; Dr J.O. Myers, 92-3; North Craven Building Preservation Trust, 71; North Yorkshire County Council, Rowley Collection, Skipton Library, 7, 21-3, 66-70, 76, 105-6, 108-9; Skipton Castle (courtesy of Sebastian Fattorini), frontispiece, 8, 11; Skipton Town Council, 6; Thornton-in-Lonsdale Church, 121; George Walker (*The Costume of Yorkshire*, 1814), 27-8, 32, 63; William Westall (1817), 49, 50, 51, 52; Godfrey Wilson, 37; Author's Collection: 26, 29, 30-1, 36, 39, 43-4, 53-5, 57-9, 65, 73-5, 77-83, 85-6, 94, 96-7, 100-104, 107, 111, 113, 116-7, 120, 122-5, 128, 131-4, 136-8, 140, 149. Uncredited photographs are by the author.

Overview

Skipton evolved from *Sceaptun* (sheep town), which at the time of Domesday was a modest settlement in an estate owned by the Saxon earl Edwin. Skipton lay in a loop of the Eller Beck, a tributary of the River Aire, and initially was less prosperous than neighbouring settlements with access to the *ings* (water meadows) of the flood plain. Skipton's importance dates from Norman times, when Robert de Romille built his castle – a motte and bailey construction – on an outcrop of rock that, on its north side, rose sheer from the beck.

The district of Craven was, according to *The Place-names of the West Riding of Yorkshire* (1961), a Domesday wapentake and later an archdeaconry. It is assumed to have a Celtic origin, associated with the Welsh *crag* (garlic), though Thomas Dunham Whitaker, author of *History of Craven*, and others preferred the allusion to 'land of crags'. J. Radford Thomson, in *Guide to the District of Craven* (1879), believed the name was derived from 'the stony rock'. The geology of Craven is spectacular. The largest outcrop of limestone in the land presents to the view vast areas of 'pavement' – flat grey rock weathered into deep clefts. The Craven Fault, a throw of some 5,000ft, brought the millstone grit on the south side down to the level of the Great Scar limestone with dramatic effect.

Whernside is the highest hill in Craven but isolated flat-topped Ingleborough, presiding over its little group of fells, is showier. The publication of an article about the mountain in *The Gentleman's Magazine* (1761) brought many tourists to the area. John Ruskin, traversing Chapel-le-Dale on a windy day, looked at the steep side of Ingleborough and wondered how the mountain could stand without rocking. In all, nine of Craven's peaks extend above the 2,000ft contour, nurturing the headwaters of three great Yorkshire rivers. The Aire, formed by a meeting of two becks just south of the village of Malham, takes an easterly course and, with the Wharfe, forms part of the Humber outfall.

The valleys of the westward-flowing Ribble and eastward-flowing Aire created what became known as the Aire Gap, the easiest crossing of the Pennines. The presence of the Gap enhanced the importance of the town. The Aire was described by the historian William Camden (1590) as being 'winding and crooked'. He passed over it seven times in half an hour on a straight road so that the river seemed at first doubtful 'whether it should run forwards into the Sea, or return into its Spring.'

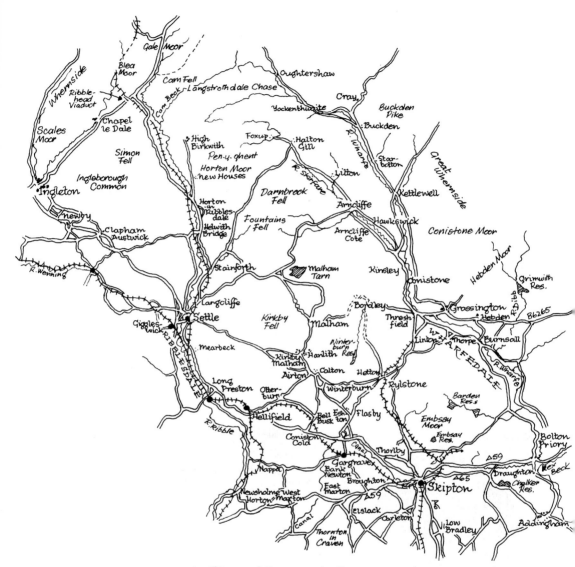

1   *Skipton and Craven map by Christine Denmead.*

Fossils in the limestone tell a 360 million-year-old story of life in a clear and shallow sea. A range of bright green mounds from around Cracoe to Thorpe is rich in fossils and the names of these reef knolls form a litany – Skelterton, Carden, Buttershaw, Langerton, Stebden, Elbolton and Kail. Bastions of the limestone country include the bow-shaped Malham Cove and the rift of Gordale Scar, where cliffs overhang, having been scoured by a mighty rush of glacial melt-water. Kilnsey Crag, at the junction of Littondale and Wharfedale, has a prominent overhang left when a glacier, in the fourth glacial epoch, cut into the side of the crag without overtopping it.

Potholes and caves honeycomb hills that look substantial from a distance. Gaping Gill, on Ingleborough, is a yawning hole leading into a chamber that has the size and grand proportions of a cathedral. The associated Ingleborough Cave, in Clapdale, was found when workmen employed by the Farrers of Ingleborough Hall broke through a stalagmite barrier. An extensive cave system, now lit by electricity, was, in the remembrance of the author, explored in the company of Arnold Brown. He carried a hissing paraffin lamp, each visitor being provided with candles on a quaint three-pronged holder. With the large key of the cave, Arnold played a tune of sorts on a set of stalactites.

The sound of rushing water competes with the bleating of sheep as becks and rivers deal with a moderately heavy rainfall. At Ingleton Glens the main feature is Thornton Force, pouring over a lip of limestone into a deep pool. The beck that flows into Alum Pot, in North Ribblesdale, flows *under* the river Ribble, from which it is separated by a belt of glacial clay, bubbling up on the other side and and flowing into the Ribble from the side opposite its source. Stainforth Force, also on the Ribble, offers a supreme test for salmon on their spawning run. Edward Elgar, the composer friend of Charles William Buck, a medical practitioner living at

2 *Old-time potholer. The lightweight ladder replaced a type made of hemp with wooden rungs.*

3 *Low cloud over Kilnsey Crag, Wharfedale.*

Giggleswick, was fond of watching water tumble off the local crags and had a framed picture of Stainforth Force clipped from a newspaper.

Victoria Cave, above Settle, excavated in Victorian days, yielded the bones of animals associated with an inter-glacial period and, at a higher level, traces of such cold weather fauna as reindeer and Arctic fox. Grazed by sheep for centuries, the landscape was stripped of its former wooded aspect. Storey, the Gargrave poet, wrote:

> There was a time when Craven saw
> From Bingley unto Oughtershaw
> One forest stretch o'er hill and dale
> Unlimited by wall or pale.

Nowadays walls made without a dab of mortar form a futuristic pattern on the Craven landscape. A drystone wall consists of two walls, standing side by side. The structure, tapering with increased height, is bound together by throughstones. The gap is infilled using small stones and is finished off with a row of capstones. William Bray, riding to Malham in 1777 when the enclosure movement was under way, saw pastures that 'have been lately divided by stone walls of about two yards high, one yard wide at the bottom, lessening to a foot at the top'. He heard that a man might build a stretch about seven yards long in a single day, being paid 'from 20d. to 2s.'. An additional cost was incurred by the delivery of stone, though it was rarely carried far. A Craven wall is by its composition an indicator of the underlying geology.

4   *In the East Passage, Gaping Gill, on the flanks of Ingleborough.*

Such a landscape bred a hardy, resourceful type of person who did well in exile but did not forget the native heath. An example was William Craven, who was born in a cottage at Appletreewick and reared in modest circumstances. He hitched a lift to London, was apprenticed as a draper, and prospered in the trade to such good effect that in 1610 he became Lord Mayor of London and was knighted in the following year. Sir William, ever mindful of his native Wharfedale, paid for the road linking Appletreewick and Burnsall, and at Burnsall he restored the church and founded a grammar school.

The town of Skipton overlooks the Aire Gap, a natural routeway through the Pennines dividing this uplift into two virtually equal parts. (The name 'Pennines' dates from a literary forgery of the 18th century. Charles Bertram (1723-65), who taught English at the Naval College at Copenhagen, filled in some slack time by devising a fictional account of Britain at the time of the Roman Empire. When published, it was purported to be the work of Richard of Cirencester, a monk of Westminster Abbey who lived in the 14th century. Bertram called the 'spine' of England *Alpes Penina* and so 'Pennines' passed into general use.) Skipton had a tucked-away location. When John Wesley first saw it, while considering a proposition to become master at the local grammar school, he confided to his mother, in a letter written in March 1727, that Skipton lay in a little vale. The place was 'so pent up between two hills that is scarcely accessible on any side; so that you can expect little company from without, and within there is none at all.' To another stranger, Thomas Gray (1762), this was 'a pretty, large market town in a valley with one very broad street gently sloping downwards from the castle.' Arthur and Elisabeth Raistrick, who in a booklet published in 1930 assessed the site value of Skipton, referred in their introduction to two natural features – the gritstone moors that virtually ringed the town and a 'plexus of small valleys'. The valleys met in lowland almost entirely occupied by glacial lake deposits and by boulder-clay in the form of drumlins.

5 *Looking down on Gordale Scar, the water-eroded gorge at the head of Malhamdale.*

6 *To the Fields. Horses on Mill Bridge, an etching by Kenneth Holmes.*

Holy Trinity Church (pictured above) forms a striking headpiece to the High Street, which is aligned north-south. The castle is a little off-set, to the north-east. The church, which dates from about 1120, began to take on its present form about the year 1300. At the time of the Dissolution it was held by Bolton Priory in Wharfedale. Bolton had been the place of interment for the Cliffords, but after the Dissolution the vault was disused. Henceforth they were laid to rest in the church at Skipton, the living of which had passed to the Dean and Chapter of Christ Church, Oxford.

Nine of the fabulous Cliffords, who sustained vast estates in Craven and Westmorland, have their last resting-place in vaults under the chancel. In the 1870s the Duke of Devonshire paid for their restoration, under the superintendence of Sir Gilbert Scott. At the time of the restoration, several brasses, missing since the siege of Skipton Castle, were recovered from a house at Thorlby and restored to their original positions. The tombs glow with colour.

Skipton's main street has kept its basic medieval design, with a few buildings flanking it. There were also stone setts for stock market purposes. The livestock market was transferred to Jerry Croft in 1906, since when the setts have been occupied by market stalls. Houses alongside the street presided over strips of land, with attendant outbuildings and gardens. A land shortage led to their development for habitations, and thus was created a pattern of yards and ginnels. These were not devised, as many were to suppose, for easy defence against rampaging Scots. Congestion in the older parts of Skipton was relieved when industry became concentrated on the south side of the town.

Situated at a communications node, Skipton is known as the 'Gateway to the Dales'. It occupies a prime site on the northern edge of a great industrial belt extending as far south as Birmingham. Northwards, for ninety miles and more, are valleys which the Norse folk called 'dales'. The Cliffords and their successors, the earls of Thanet, steadfastly refused to release land on a long-term basis and the growth of industry in the town was retarded. While large tracts of the West Riding and north-east Lancashire were industrialised, Old Skipton remained rural – pastoral, indeed – and it was not until the late 18th or early 19th centuries that a major industry, textiles, arrived, thus increasing the urban population. The big mills operated to the south, beside a canal that delivered cheap coal to their back doors. When the textile trade collapsed, most of the mills were converted into flats. The most imposing commercial building is now the head office of the Skipton Building Society, which provides jobs in the town for over one thousand people.

Up country from Skipton, where – as dale-country author Halliwell Sutcliffe was to write – the lean lands meet the sky, is a landscape of farms, hamlets and villages. Chiang Yee, a Chinese visitor to Parcevall Hall in the late 1930s, wrote of the spring sunshine 'pouring down on the hills with their white and green and brown, making them look warm and drowsy'. Two populous settlements are Grassington in Wharfedale and Settle, a market town in North Ribblesdale.

Grassington (of Anglian foundation, locally known as Girston) stands on a shelf of well-drained land high above the River Wharfe. The Alcock family, the one-time owners of Grassington House, a Georgian building overlooking the partly cobbled Square, was connected with banking and promoted the turnpike road between Grassington and Pateley Bridge. A stone bridge spanning the Wharfe, properly known as Linton Bridge, succeeded a timber structure in 1603. The parish church, on the Linton bank of the river, presides over the townships of Linton, Grassington, Threshfield and Hebden.

The Rev. Bailey J. Harker, in a guide to Grassington entitled *The Buxton of Yorkshire* (1890), was catering to tourism so drew the visitor's attention to the horse-drawn omnibuses that connected Skipton with Grassington and Hebden. Tourists, anglers and cyclists would find *The Foresters' Arms Hotel* the proverbial 'home from home', while the Old Hall, Threshfield, offered trout fishing in the Wharfe – and the use of an excellent bath. By the dawn of the 20th century, when lead mining had waned and around half the local dwellings had been vacated, a single-track railway was laid from Skipton to Grassington, bringing the rural delights of Upper Wharfedale to within commuting distance of Bradford and, to a lesser extent, Leeds. The recently vacated cottages were available for the new settlers.

Thomas Pennant, an 18th-century visitor to Settle, described it as 'a small town in a little vale, exactly resembling a shabby French town ... It has a small trade in knit-worsted stockings, which are made here from two to five shillings a pair.' A limestone knoll, Castleberg, dominates the oldest parts of the town. Isaac Newton made a laborious journey to Langcliffe, near Settle, to meet Dawson, an old friend, although the apple that gave him an insight into the earth's gravitational pull was observed elsewhere. Langcliffe Hall was also a country residence of Geoffrey Dawson, for many years editor of *The Times*. He was born Geoffrey Robinson at Skipton and changed his name by deed poll to inherit the Langcliffe estate.

The town has an astonishing 17th-century building known as The Folly, part of which is now a museum. A local café, *Ye Old Naked Man*, was formerly an inn, its name possibly a skit on excesses in clothing fashions (there is a *Naked Woman* at Langcliffe). The scenic Settle-Carlisle railway crosses the town on imposing viaducts and embankments. Old Settle was conspicuously a place of ginnels, alleys and narrow streets. Now its appearance is more open and the town has experienced the architectural equivalent of middle-aged spread – an infilling of open land with council houses and bungalows. Townhead, a Victorian mansion presiding over park-like country beyond the church, was demolished and modern housing covers the hillside. The river is the division between Settle and Giggleswick. The last-named village has a celebrated public school, the domed chapel of which – a gift of Walter Morrison, 'the Craven millionaire', in Victoria's Diamond Jubilee year – breaks the skyline, its appearance bringing praise from most people. A former deputy headmaster compared it with 'a jelly mould'.

Wharfedale, one of the most attractive valleys in England – a combination of moorland, woodland, river and mellowed ruins – is steeped in romance. Craven's most written about and painted monastic ruins stand at Bolton in Wharfedale, the adjacent nave saved from destruction at the Dissolution and retained as the parish church. The Priory gateway (it was not an Abbey, as the postal address suggests) is incorporated in Bolton Hall, a residence of the dukes of Devonshire. The lives of the monks were not always as contemplative and sunlit as one often supposes. The peace of Bolton was shattered in 1318 and 1319 by raiding parties of Scots. In that same decade were natural disasters that almost wrecked the economy, heavy rain ruining the corn harvest and resulting in a lack of hay and sodden pastures for the stock. The 3,000-strong sheep flock was culled by over two-thirds. Wheat purchased by the monks cost five times the normal price.

Yet, centuries later, the melancholy beauty of a partly ruined abbey had, according to John Ruskin, a great influence on the art of the water-colourist Turner. Landseer, the favourite artist of Queen Victoria, arrived wearing a maroon shooting-coat to make sketches for his large painting of 'Bolton Abbey in the Olden Time', a painting commissioned by the Duke of Devonshire and seen by patrons of the Royal Academy in 1834. Exhibited in London before finding a permanent home at Chatsworth, the canvas was as effective as a tourist poster in bringing to the Yorkshire Dales seekers after beauty and antiquity. Nathaniel Hawthorne saw the ruined priory 'in the green lap of protecting hills, beside a stream, and with peace and fertility looking down on every side'.

Gritstone moors, as on the Bolton Abbey estate in Wharfedale, have been well managed for the benefit of red grouse and for those with the leisure and means to shoot them, a sport which developed speedily with the coming of the railways. 'Swiddening', or the regular burning of strips of moorland to encourage the growth

7   *Skipton High Street, as it was in the inter-war years. Lime trees were planted to mark the Diamond Jubilee of Victoria in 1897.*

of young shoots, benefits grouse, upland waders such as the curlew, and sheep, the special Craven type being the Dales-bred. Royalty attended the grouse shoots organised by successive dukes of Devonshire. Old people were fond of recalling when King George V made a stately arrival for the grouse shooting. On Sunday he walked from Bolton Hall to the Priory church to attend a service. One of the bystanders is said to have described him as 'a little-ish fellow with gingery whiskers: a gruff sort of man, but kind to children'.

Back at Skipton, by-passes were made to reduce the traffic pressure on the High Street. This thoroughfare is, nonetheless, still busy, Skipton having become one of the wealthiest towns in the country. Heavy industry has been replaced by 'tertiary-sector activities', by retailing, offices, shops and innumerable market stalls that bring in visitors by the thousand, many from the towns of east Lancashire. The accent is now on cheap homes and badly needed office space. Victoria Mill, once devoted to paper production, is composed of luxury flats but presents a traditional face to the town. Belle Vue Mill, of the Dewhurst family, situated in a conservation area adjacent to the Leeds and Liverpool Canal, is earmarked for a hundred new homes together with commercial properties.

Skipton auction mart was transferred from a site off Broughton Road to one at the edge of the town and the old site is now occupied by a supermarket, which preserves in its design the circular form of the sales ring. Craven, long renowned for its grazing land and for the quality of its sheep and cattle, and especially for its limestone country, is the subject of a limestone project that harks back to an old system of stock management. By reducing sheep numbers and introducing hardy upland cattle in the right balance, the sward is evenly grazed. Cattle take the coarser grasses left by the sheep. The international biodiversity of limestone country is recognised by the designation of two Special Areas of Conservation – the Ingleborough complex and the Craven limestone complex, representing 27,420 acres. It includes eight Sites of Special Scientific Interest, and National Nature Reserves at Ingleborough and Malham Tarn.

Chapter 1

A Place of Defence

Skipton, an unimportant Saxon hamlet, took on a regional significance with the arrival of Robert de Romille and his family. Earl Edwin, the Saxon owner, had been permitted to retain his lands, residing at Bolton in Wharfedale, but, having joined a revolt in support of a Danish invasion in 1071, he was slain in battle and his estates were forfeited to the king. Entries in the Domesday Survey of 1086 classified these estates as *Terra Regis*. They were also designated as 'waste', possibly as a result of the Conqueror's Harrying of the North. Robert de Romille added the Craven properties to land he possessed at Harewood in Yorkshire and to his estates in Dorset and Devon.

Requiring a fortified building – a place of defence – his attention focused on Skipton and, more precisely, on the huge rock above the wooded gorge of Eller Beck, a rock that would inhibit any attack from the north. The first castle would

8   *Hawkins' engraving of Skipton Castle.*

9 *Base of a monastic cross in Mastiles Lane, which extended from Kilnsey to Malham Moor.*

be of the motte and bailey type. The motte, a mound of earth ringed by a timber palisade, protected my lord's living quarters and contained separate accommodation for his guards. Within the adjacent bailey, which was an equally well-protected area, were quarters for retainers, as well as stables and stores. Strategically placed between the castles of Clitheroe and Knaresborough, Skipton overlooked the Aire Gap and was at the point of convergence of several important roads. With a garrison of cavalrymen, Romille was ever ready to serve his king. He also had the means to subdue any fretful natives who decided to test his strength.

Robert's daughter, Cecily, married William de Meschines, lord of the barony of Copeland in Cumberland. Having treasures enough on earth, they set about ensuring they might also have divine goodwill in the next world. In the year 1120 they enabled a group of Augustinian canons to establish a priory at nearby Embsay, for 'the health of our souls and those of our ancestors and successors'. When Alice de Romille, a second daughter, inherited Copeland, she exchanged Bolton for land elsewhere and the 'black canons' of Embsay could now quit the high ground for a sheltered, well-watered place by the River Wharfe. The canons, keeping to a strict religious rule, employed men to work their farms. In 1135 the Scots under King David swept through northern England and a detachment of the army, led by David's nephew William Fitz Duncan, took Skipton. William married Alice de Romille.

Most of the hill land of Craven came into monastic hands during the 12th and 13th centuries. The monks kept a huge stock of sheep to the detriment of the native deer and of trees, the timber being unable to regenerate naturally. Cistercians who had settled at Fountains in the valley of the Skell near Ripon had their principal grange at Kilnsey, which they received from the benevolent Alice de Romille in 1156. Kilnsey was a great sheep grange, with chapel, mills, houses and sheepfolds. Three lay brethren were in permanent residence. At shearing time, flocks from the moors of Malham and Kilnsey and also from Littondale were driven to Kilnsey to be shorn. The wool, transported across the moors to the Abbey in ox-driven wains, clothed the monks, any surplus being exported to Italy.

Also having territorial rights in Craven were the monks of Byland, Salley (Sawley) and Furness Abbeys, and among the up-and-coming families were the Tempests, who owned three carucates in Bracewell and two bovates in Skipton. John Tempest of Bracewell purchased the manor of Broughton in 1316.

When another Cecily married William le Gross, Earl of Albemarle, two great estates were combined. King Henry contrived that Hawise, Cecily's only child, would marry William de Mandeville, Earl of Essex. On his death, pressure was put on Hawise to marry William de Fortibus, which she did despite his social inferiority, though he had the wit and acquired means to update Skipton Castle. The marriage lasted for less than five years and William died in 1195. Hawise, widowed for a second time, was married off by King Richard to the socially acceptable Baldwin de Bethune. When he died in 1212, Hawise – weary of arranged marriages – paid King John a substantial sum so that she might not be asked to marry again!

After her death, royal bailiffs occupied her properties until the King permitted them to be inherited by William de Fortibus, Earl of Albemarle. His place in history was assured when he became one of the 25 signatories of Magna Carta. Skipton Castle now took on a grand appearance through a building scheme put into effect about 1227. Well-dressed stone went into walls that were up to 11 feet thick. Four round towers and curtain walls protected a stone gatehouse that had been built by William's father and was now absorbed by the general scheme. A central courtyard or inner bailey was enclosed.

Friends visiting Skipton Castle marvelled at a great hall, the dimensions of which were 55ft by 25ft, the roof being supported by hammer-beams. On formal occasions, the family occupied a dais. Should greater privacy be desired, they entered a withdrawing room from which their private apartments might be accessed. The castle had easy-to-maintain toilets which discharged directly into Eller Beck. William died in 1241 and his successor, another William, breathed his last in 1260. For half a century, Skipton Castle and its estate were in royal hands, and then it was leased to Henry de Lacy in 1308 at a rent of 200 marks per annum. The fabric had been allowed to deteriorate and in the park mares greatly outnumbered what had been a prime stock of fallow deer. Oak trees from local woods had been sold for iron forging.

The Romille connection and that of their descendants in Craven ended in 1274 with the death without issue of Countess Aveline de Fortibus. In 1310 there began what was to be the long occupation of Skipton by the Clifford family. On their arrival in England, the family was named Pont or Punt, serving on the Welsh Marches. The Clifford name was taken from Clifford Castle in Herefordshire, which they secured by marriage. When Robert de Clifford (1274-1314), son of Roger de Clifford and Isabella de Veteripont, was granted the Castle and land in the manor of Skipton, they were valued at £200 per annum, half of which was for life and half in tail (entailed to his heirs). Subsequently the whole estate was granted in tail, though Edward II retained the issues of the Castle and manor in excess of £200. When the grant was further enlarged, Robert secured 'the Castle, Manor and lands of Skipton, with the Knights fees, advowsons, homages, demesnes and liberties as fully as the Earls of Albemarle held the same'.

Robert was already a considerable landowner, having a Vipont inheritance comprising the Barony of Westmorland, which had been created by William Rufus. Summoned to Parliament as a baron, Robert established a hereditary peerage. His many duties included Warden of the Scottish Marches and Captain of Carlisle. Though he spent long periods away from home, he would have been content to know that his family were living well back from the main action.

In 1311 Skipton was of modest size. Here were two corn mills valued at £13 6s. 8d., a fulling mill (10s.) and a dyehouse (20s.). The 247 acres of arable land were valued at 10d. an acre and 68 acres of meadow were assessed at 2s. 6d. an acre. A further sum of about 50s. was accounted for by two oxgangs of land and meadow, with meadow and pasturage dispersed among the fields. Ten tofts and burgages and some rough pasture lay outside the town fields. The greater part of the town's wealth came from market tolls, freehold rents and court fees.

In three busy years, Robert de Clifford re-aligned the approach to Skipton Castle, adjusting the entry point from west to south. Strong perimeter defences included a massive gatehouse set to the east of Holy Trinity Church, its two round towers bringing the number in the Castle to four. A dry moat, with drawbridge and portcullis, were part of the new defensive scheme.

Early Cliffords died violently. Robert, slain at Bannockburn in 1314, was

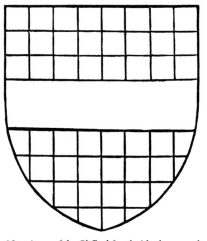

10   Arms of the Clifford family (checky, or and azure, a fess gules).

interred at Shap Abbey in Westmorland. His son, Roger, was among the barons in an unsuccessful rising in 1322. Some doubt exists about the manner of his death. He was either hanged in chains at York or, according to Mathew Hale, was reprieved 'by reason of his great wounds, he being a dying man'. Robert (1305-44) preferred the frivolities of court life to the rough experiences of the field. His successors were men of action: Robert (1331-52?) fought at Crecy and another Roger (1335-90) engaged in the wars against France and Scotland; Thomas (1364-92) was slain in Germany and John (1389-1422) died at the Siege of Meaux; Thomas (1415-55) served in the French wars and, on the outbreak of the Wars of the Roses, was slain while fighting on the Lancashire side at the Battle of St Albans.

John Lord Clifford (1430-61), keen to avenge his father, was incriminated in the murder of the young Earl of Rutland after the Battle of Wakefield, an unlikely tale considering that the 'young' son was a

11   *Francis Clifford (1559-1641).*

youth of 17 years who almost certainly fell fighting. It was not customary to wreak vengeance on the children of the fallen; the tables might easily be turned. Just before the Battle of Towton, an unknown archer shot John in the throat.

His estates were attainted and the Honour of Skipton was granted first to Sir William Stanley and then, in 1475, to the future King Richard III, then Duke of Gloucester. John's son, Henry (1453-1523), in danger from his enemies because of his father's alleged barbarity, was exiled. The poet Wordsworth erroneously set Henry's 'hidden years' on the wild fells of Cumberland:

> Our Clifford was a happy youth,
> And thankful through a weary time,
> That brought him up to manhood's prime.
> Again he wanders forth at will,
> And tends a flock from hill to hill:
> His garb was humble; ne'er was seen
> Such garb with such a noble mien.

Winifred Haward, who spent her later years in Littondale, found the 'shepherd story' in Hall's Chronicle, written in 1548 – a quarter of a century after the death

12 *Skipton Parish Church, resting place for generations of Cliffords.*

of Henry. The story was 'lifted' from Hall by Holinshed, then Shakespeare took it from him. A century later, Lady Anne Clifford included it in her history of the Cliffords. The story was attached to Henry Clifford because – theorised Winifred Haward – the shepherd was a symbol of the simple virtues, especially in societies where the rich were enjoying a highly elaborate and artificial culture, and Henry fitted this picture. The truth behind his exile is that for most of the 'hidden years' he lived as a simple esquire on his grandfather's estates at Londesborough, in the East Riding of Yorkshire.

Restored to his estates in 1484, the Shepherd Lord married Anne, the King's cousin, in 1487, and housed her in new apartments set in the inner court. They had a large family. Henry spent much of his time at Barden Tower, a former hunting lodge in Wharfedale. The Tower's function as a lodge in the Forest of Barden had declined as much of the area was settled in small freeholds. Lodges generally became large farms and land was assarted from the forest for their cattle and crops. Henry made the building a grander place and created nearby a chapel and priest's house. A modern biographer, Richard T. Spence, described him as 'robust, pious and scholarly', with a peripatetic household of between 50 and 60 people who moved from place to place in the north and occasionally bore down on the Court of Westminster. Hunting was an enjoyable diversion.

Raistrick, writing about Barden in *The Dalesman*, stated that the Barden accounts of 1510 did not confirm the general picture of Henry as a studious recluse, shut off from the world. Barden received a tun of wine from York, a swan from Appleby, a wild boar and other stuff, salt fish from Hartlepool and items for green ginger and treacle. Music and entertainment were part of Barden life. Payments were made for strings for a fiddle, for a bagpipe and for a livery jacket for young Long the

13   *Brass on the tomb of Henry Clifford, Skipton Parish Church.*

Piper. Further costs were payment for minstrels, for drums and shawmes, for players from Halifax on St Thomas's Day and to the 'lord of misrule', the leader in many pleasant festivities.

Henry enjoyed the company of the Bolton monks. In contrast to his lifestyle, they lived mainly on bread, pottage and a gallon of ale per man per day made from local oats, supplemented by dairy products, trout from the Wharfe and herring imported via a tedious land journey from the Yorkshire coast. The Shepherd Lord had a busy but peaceful existence, commuting from one part of his vast estates to another, until in 1513 he led a party of his Craven levies with guns to Flodden Field. Among his trophies of that battle, in which the Craven men distinguished themselves, were three brass culverins, each 13 feet long and weighing over two tons, which had belonged to James IV, the Scottish King. At Skipton, they were set at the approach to the Drum Tower in the outer bailey, and there they remained until the Castle was slighted over a century later.

Henry provided funds for the construction of a West Tower at Bolton Priory, a task begun in 1520 by Prior Moone. He contracted in 1513 for his heir, another Henry, to be married to Margaret Percy, daughter of Henry, 5th Earl of Northumberland, who gave her 'a good portion of lands'. Henry was created Earl of Cumberland in

14   *Brass on the slab of a Clifford tomb, Skipton Parish Church.*

1525, and ten years later he was contemplating the forthcoming marriage of his son, also Henry, a budding 2nd Earl of Cumberland, to Lady Eleanor Brandon, the niece of Henry VIII. In about five months, an east wing on a scale fit for such a fine lady was added to Skipton Castle. A multi-storeyed Octagonal Tower came into being with three spacious rooms complete with fireplaces. A long gallery – a French idea which was just becoming popular in England – linked Eleanor's domestic quarters in the Tower with the Drum Towers. The gallery became a place of recreation for the ladies, offering views to the south over the Aire valley and to the north of the woodland that lay beyond Eller Beck.

In the religious and social rebellion known as the Pilgrimage of Grace (1536), Clifford stood firm and kept the rebels at bay with the Castle's great ordnance. Lady Eleanor and her family, who were staying at Bolton Priory when the rebellion occurred, were ushered in secret to the safety of the Castle. In the following year, Henry, 2nd Earl of Cumberland, gained the Percy fee, the second great seigniory in Craven, dating back to William de Percy at the time of the Conquest. With the fee came lordships, deer reserves and timber resources in the Forest of Langstrothdale.

George, 3rd Earl of Cumberland (1558-1608), and his family spent little time at Skipton, their main residence being in London. Encouraged by Queen Elizabeth, he became a buccaneer. The Queen took a substantial share of any bounty with no cost to herself, although George was rewarded with the Garter. In pursuit of Spanish loot and royal favour, he neglected his family, sold off some of his northern possessions to finance his buccaneering and, in due course, was provided with a spectacular tomb in Holy Trinity, Skipton. Cyril Harrington, writing in *The Dalesman*, was to describe the last resting place of the man he called 'Old Buccaneer George'

15 *Barden Tower, Wharfedale, a favourite retreat of the Shepherd Lord (Henry Clifford).*

16   *Bolton Priory, once occupied by Augustinian canons.*

as 'the most breathtaking thing in the whole town ... That most arrogant display of heraldry, and the disdainful simplicity of its background, seem to challenge the very altar itself.'

After George's death, a great lawsuit ensued between Francis, his younger brother, and Anne, who was George's only child. The Clifford estates were entailed in the direct line, regardless of sex. Unaccountably, in the will Anne was by-passed, and a bitter family feud developed with the Honour of Skipton at stake. Francis, 4th Earl of Cumberland (1559-1641), who had been born in the Castle, and his son Henry, 5th Earl (1591-1643), successively claimed the title. In 1606, just before he took up residence, Francis had the Castle refurbished at enormous cost. Windows were glazed and the roof re-leaded. When he moved here in the summer of 1608, the event was celebrated with feasting and entertainment on a grand scale. The interest of Francis in the castle dwindled following the death of his wife, Countess Grissell, in 1613.

Skipton was the setting for special family gatherings until the outbreak of the Civil War. In that conflict, which broke out in 1642, the Lord of Skipton was Henry Clifford. Being also the Lord Lieutenant of the County of York, he executed the King's Commission and should have commanded the Royalist forces in Yorkshire. Alas for him, but not for Skipton, he was 'much decayed in the vigour of his body and mind and unfit for the activity which the season required'. The leadership fell into the more competent hands of the Earl of Newcastle. The defence of the Castle was organised by Sir John Mallory, the Governor, and Major Hughes, the Lieutenant Governor. They commanded about 300 men.

17 *Gateway of Skipton Castle, an unusual view from the Castle grounds.*

18 *Conduit Court, Skipton Castle. The conduit provided fresh water.*

Skipton was the last Royalist bastion in northern England to yield. A siege of over three years began in 1642 but was not one of constant harassment. During the first two years, the Parliamentary force was content to keep the Royalists in check. The Royalists made frequent sallies, some of which led to bloody scuffles, then the Castle walls were breached by cannon fire and the Castle was surrendered on generous terms in December 1645. The Parliamentary generals in the north, Lambert and Fairfax, friends of the Clifford family, had kept damage to Skipton Castle to a minimum. Holy Trinity Church had its steeple riddled with cannon balls and the tombs of Henry, 1st Earl and Francis Lord Clifford were defaced. Parliament took Castle, cannons and provisions, but

19   *Lady Anne Clifford (1589-1675).*

the honour of the garrison remained intact. Led by their Governor, the erstwhile garrison marched out of the Castle with trumpets sounding, colours flying and drums beating, and prisoners were released. Royalist supporters had free passage to side with King Charles I at one of his garrisons – or to return home. Sick or wounded men were tended in good accommodation at Skipton until they recovered.

Oliver Cromwell ordered that the Castle should be 'slighted', its defences so weakened it would not be a future threat. The writer of a guidebook published by John Garnett at Skipton in 1853 refers to a tradition at Broughton Hall that, in 'the last civil wars', a son of the family was shot on the lawn. The village of Broughton had been so completely pillaged of common utensils by the hostile garrisons of Skipton and at Thornton-in-Craven that 'an old helmet travelled from house to house for the purpose of boiling broth and pottage'.

In 1617 an award issued by James I settled the dispute with Lady Anne Clifford (1589-1675), but she refused to subscribe to it. On the death of Francis and Henry, Anne came triumphantly into her own, moving north to take over the family estates and keep the medieval spirit alive in a progressive age, almost becoming a queen in the Craven and Westmorland dales. As Cyril Harrington has written, 'We may

20   *Signature of Lady Anne Clifford.*

surely count Anne Clifford as of the Middle Ages in spite of the fact that she was contemporary with Milton ... Despite Countess Anne, however, the renaissance was an accomplished fact.'

Lady Anne was 54 years old when she came into her inheritance and lived to enjoy her Clifford heritage for a further 32 years. Patrick Eyres summed up her restless energy in *Lady Anne's Way*, a companion to an exhibition held at Bolton Abbey in the spring of 1985. In the 15 years between 1649 and 1664 she 'restored her estates, established a regional Welfare State and generated employment through extensive building works. She rebuilt castles and churches, built almshouses and erected monuments throughout her estates in Westmorland and Yorkshire. Her zeal was such that she became a legend in her own lifetime.'

Skipton Castle gatehouse was rebuilt after the Civil War battering, and – ignoring threats from Cromwell, who quietly admired her spirit – Anne set about restoring other parts of the building. Its military use was lessened when a sloping, slated roof replaced the strong, flat one on which cannon had reposed. Additional glazed windows were provided in rebuilt walls that were less bulky than the old walls. In 1659 Anne had a yew tree planted in the Conduit Court, whose name referred to the water supply. Inscribed tablets and the initials AP appeared on virtually everything she built or restored, leaving no one in doubt who had done the work. On her death, the Honour passed to the Tufton family, first to her four grandsons, successively earls of Thanet, the last of whom died in 1729.

The Tuftons, who lived in the south, neglected Skipton Castle, which became dilapidated. In 1792 the Hon. John Byng recorded in his diary an unflattering description. The castle was 'a most inconvenient, miserable, tattered place, with neither beauty of building nor pleasing antiquity but a melancholy wretchedness of bad old rooms, some miserable tapestries and some basely neglected pictures'. It was no longer a place of defence.

Chapter 2

Trade and Commerce

The earliest known representation of Skipton is a sketch of *c.*1720 made by Samuel Buck, who was employed by John Warburton to illustrate a history of Yorkshire. Buck viewed the town from Park Hill, thus showing Skipton from the north. A glimpse of the east side of the northern end of the main street shows houses that are tightly packed along the frontage, some houses offering to view just their gable-ends. The main street that for centuries *was* Skipton would have had a handsome headpiece in Holy Trinity Church, successor to the building of the early 12th century. The church took its present form in the 14th and 15th centuries, with much repair work needed after its Civil War battering.

Skipton had a market prior to 1189. In that year Alice de Romille gave to the canons of Bolton the right to trade in the town free of tolls. King John granted to Baldwin de Betun a charter for a market and fairs. Skipton was then little more than its broad street, fronted by houses of modest size, each with its long and narrow garden plot. The Market Place, the lower part of the street, adjoined the Middle Row. Sheep Market Street, later known simply as Sheep Street, lay to the west. Skipton's evolution as a market town was complete with Market Cross.

21 *Skipton High Street with sheep pens. The town was named after sheep.*

The market took place on Saturdays throughout the year. There were two fairs, 'at the ffeast of St Martyn for eight dayes and at the ffeast of St James for eight dayes'. Skipton's livestock fair, gained in 1597, was held fortnightly from Easter to Christmas. Ten more fairs were added to the tally in 1756. In 1249 Settle received its market charter from Henry III, via Henry de Percy, becoming an important focal point for Ribblesdale and much of the rich Craven lowlands. (Its Tuesday market endures.) In 1310 permission was granted for a two-day fair at Appletreewick in Wharfedale, a grant that was renewed by Edward III. (The fair, noted for the quality of its sheep, was to survive until the mid-19th century.)

Dawson, in his *History of Skipton*, reviewed the value of agricultural produce at the beginning of the 14th century. A sack of wool, 26 stones of 14 pounds each, was worth about £6. Black wool sold at 5s. the stone. A sheep sold for 1s., a cow might be purchased for 7s. 4d. and an ox for 13s. 4d. Dawson quotes the wages of a labourer at 1d. or 1½d. a day. As the 16th century drew to a close, the town's cattle fair was widely known, and now George, Earl of Cumberland obtained a charter for a fair to be held every second Tuesday.

22   *Cattle Market, Skipton High Street. This was transferred to Jerry Croft in 1906.*

23 *Market Day, Skipton High Street, the width of which was determined by its market status.*

24 *Horse Fair, Skipton High Street, 1920s.*

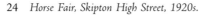

By the end of the century, 13 families were directly engaged in the manufacture or sale of clothing and cloth goods in a cottage industry complete with weaving, dyeing and fulling. Two Flemish weavers, Peter de Braband and his son, were active. Between 1717 and 1725 leases were granted to wool combers and weavers, who were building cottages along the Newmarket. The list of rentals was augmented a few years later by both shalloon and worsted weavers.

25   *Skipton auction mart, 1928.*

Geoffrey Rowley, a modern historian, thought that the Newmarket was possibly an overflow from the Market Place at the lower end of the High Street. Property in the Newmarket is mentioned in the will of one Christopher Lambert (1555). The 'New Markett' is among a record of the leases granted by Lady Anne Clifford in 1650. One James Dolfin, a 'linnen webster', had come into the possession of premises therein, the conditions of tenancy including payment of £5 yearly and a load of coals to the Castle. In 1675, according to W.H. Dawson, 30 men were indicted at Skipton Sessions for following the trade of butcher without having been apprenticed to it. In 1756 local fairs existed for horned cattle, sheep, horses, linen and broad cloth.

The Court Leet, a pioneering unit of local government, was at the height of its power when Anne Clifford presided over the estate, and Skipton was frequently referred to as 'the burgh'. The High Mill, near the Castle, was opened as a cotton yarn spinning mill in 1785, the rest of the manufacturers being employed in the worsted industry. In the 18th century, tolls were 'farmed', according to Dawson: in 1702 the Earl of Thanet granted to Thomas Chamberlain, of Skipton, 'the great tolls of cattle, corne, graine, wooll, and the goods sold, issueing out of the ffaires and markets within the towne of Skipton ... for a term of eleven years, in return for an annual rent of eighteen pounds of good and lawful money of England'.

Craven's damp climate having proved unsuited to arable crops, although a Corn Market was known to exist in 1655; corn was being transported to the town from Knaresborough and the Vale of York on a road system that included the Embsay valley. An alternative route, from Richmondshire, took in Coverdale to Wharfedale, though at the point of division between the two dales was Park Rash, marking an altogether-too-rapid descent into Wharfedale. Corn purchased at Skipton was 'dispersed from hence into different parts of Craven and into the north-eastern parts of Lancashire', wrote Dawson, quoting from an unnamed topographer writing sixty years before. 'Formerly scarcely a cart was to be seen in Skipton market, but now no fewer than 200 attend weekly.' This was 'partly owing to the great quantities of corn produced by the inclosure of Knaresbro' Forest'. Skipton received wool from all parts of the Craven district.

The Court Leet continued to maintain the market customs, to repair the roads and to prevent public nuisances, occasionally reinforcing their presentments with fines. Any fines were, according to Dawson, 'dropped into the coffers of the lord of the manor'. In 1727 market traders risked being fined if they set up unlicensed stalls on the 'stone setts' in the High Street (then commonly known as the Street of Skipton), or left their stalls in the streets at night. A recurrent crime in the first half of the century was the keeping of unmuzzled mastiffs 'to the great Danger and Terror of the inhabitants'.

In 1741 emphasis was laid on keeping the frontages of buildings clear of dirt. Specified were 'the Upper Street of Skipton to the Chanell or Long Causey and those in Swadford Street and Newmarket to the sides of the Causey'. Beck pollution was a common occurrence, Eller Beck being the principal sufferer. On 3 April 1743, the

26   *Langstrothdale in 1900. Skipton was the major trading place for Craven's farmstock.*

affected stretch lay at the back of the New Market. The Court records referred to Abraham Dixon and his servants who, on 1 December last, 'cast and threw into the said rivulet a large quantity of soap-sudds and other noysome and unwholesome waters and other offals, to the great noyance of the said water and all the people'. On 15 October 1745 Abraham was still washing his wool in common water and there were complaints about people erecting 'little houses upon the common rivers or water places'. Householders were presented to the Court Leet for keeping dunghills and rubbish at the front of their homes or on the highway. In 1749, 'many butchers do kill cattle … and suffer their Blood and other Offals to be thrown into the streets'.

One of the features of the story of both Skipton and Craven is good education. Ermysted's, one of the best state schools in the land, is named after Canon William Ermysted, who in 1548 drew up an endowment deed for the continuance and develop-ment of a school threatened by recent historical events; he also left monies for its maintenance and upkeep. Peter Toller, who died in 1492, is regarded as the founder, having left a bequest to a school. Ermysted had a clear view of the form the curriculum should take. In 1548, 120 boys were attending a new school under the tutelage of one Stephen Ellis, 'a good grammarian', who had become the first headmaster.

Eighteenth-century travellers arrived in 'the Street of Skipton' after descending Shode Bank from Rombald's Moor and traversing Newmarket. To Gent (1733) this was a 'beautiful town'. Thomas Gray (1762), recovering from the stresses of 'the steepest hill I ever saw a road carried over in England', found himself in 'a pretty large market town in a valley, with one very broad street, gently sloping downwards from the Castle, which stands at the head of it'. Pennant (1776) noted the existence of 'one broad street, the Church and Castle terminating the upper end'. The pillory had been removed in 1770, but stocks stood near the Market Cross, which had a stone awning. Until the end of the 18th century, sheep-stealers and others convicted of felony were publicly flogged at the Market Cross.

27   An old-time Peat Cart in Langstrothdale (from The Costume of Yorkshire).

28   *Yorkshire Horse-dealer (from The Costume of Yorkshire).*

29   *North Ribblesdale Show, Bridge End, Settle. The land was once known as the Archery Field.*

The firm of Messrs Birkbeck, Alcocks & Co., trading under the name of the Craven Banking Company, was established as a distinct banking business at Settle and Skipton in 1791. The agreement was signed by a quartet of steady-going country bankers, namely William and John Birkbeck, William Nicholson Alcock and John Peart. The obituary of William Birkbeck, who died at Linton on 6 January 1838 aged 66, appeared in the *Gentleman's Magazine*. He was said to be the first member of the Society of Friends who qualified as a Justice of the Peace. 'His interest in the success of the Mechanics Institute was scarcely less than that of his brother, Dr Birkbeck of London.' Alcock, who was born in 1789, lived to the then ripe age of 87.

30 *Goose Fair, Settle, c.1900. Geese were driven over warm tar to reinforce their webbed feet for a journey to market.*

Craven banknotes were reputable even during a major panic in 1825 when many banks closed. The partners, who were held in high esteem, obtained the goodwill of Craven farmers by featuring a cow on some of the notes. A not uncommon request when a choice of notes was offered would be 'Gie me one wi' a coo' on.' The etching was of the celebrated Craven Heifer, bred at Bolton Abbey by the Rev. William Carr; prior to 1817, all notes printed had borne a picture of Castleberg rock at Settle. In 1906 the Craven Bank was taken over by the Bank of Liverpool, and in 1918 was absorbed by Martins Bank.

Into the High Street at Skipton came cattle and sheep that had filled out their frames by grazing on Craven's limestone uplands. During the 18th century, 'black Scotch cattle', rested and fed around Malham, were more popular with the butchers than the native breeds. Cattle fairs were held on alternate Tuesdays until, in the 19th century, the day was switched to Monday. Skipton was noted for its pig market, and each autumn a horse fair took place. On market day, local people had to watch their step, if they ventured into the street at all. The filth and odours of massed animals could be almost unbearable, causing W.H. Dawson, Victorian editor of the *Craven Pioneer*, to marvel that a street market – 'an anachronism so dangerous to public health and opposed to public convenience' – should have been tolerated for so long.

The town was well endowed with inns, the oldest being the *Red Lion* (still operative after 500 years, its arched cellars giving it a whiff of antiquity). Early inns at Skipton were combined with farming, the *Red Lion* farm embracing Jerry Croft. The *Old George*, formerly the *George Inn*, is noted in a rent roll of the Castle estate in 1649, where it was described as 'one ancient burgage, two stables, one great barn, one house and cow house, one garden, one croft and backside or fold ...' The *Black Horse* was built in 1676, probably on the site of an earlier licensed house. Until the 1720s it was an alehouse called the *King's Head*. Geoffrey Rowley wrote in 1969 of the *Red Lion* looking across to the *Black Horse*, the *Old George* facing *Anderton's Bar* and the *Hole-in-the-Wall* being opposite the *Brick Hall*, which was kept as an inn from at least 1777 onwards, having a brewhouse at the back by 1727. Among the many lost inns of Skipton is the *Bear and Ragged Staff*, which in 1684 was being kept by Mary Goodgion. (The site is now occupied by Woolworths store.)

Chapter 3

A Farming Life

Archaeologists analysing human remains found in Craven caves deduce that farming in the area dates back thousands of years. Tom Lord, who farms Winskill, in limestone country near Langcliffe, has followed up the work on cave remains conducted by his grandfather, Tot, in the 1920s and 1930s. Such material has been the subject of precise radio-carbon dating by Oxford University and Mr Lord states, 'No longer can we think of upland areas such as the Yorkshire Dales as remote and backward. The radio-carbon dating evidence indicates the presence of farming communities … as early as anywhere in Britain.' The work of archaeologists implies that farming in Craven was taking place in Neolithic times, c.4,000 B.C., when clearings were made in the forest using stone axes. Within the area grazed by domesticated animals, natural regeneration of the timber was not possible. On dry limestone strips beside Ingleborough and Malham Cove early man planted corn with reasonable confidence that it might be harvested.

An insight into the farming scene in the 13th and 14th centuries was provided when Professor Kershaw analysed the accounts of Bolton Priory, where the cellarer, who was a canon, undertook the overall estate management. Oxen were bred to haul the plough, each plough needing a team of eight animals. A stud for horses was established at Bolton and land at Malham was used as summer pasture. Also at Malham were goats, from which came milk, surplus kids being allocated to the table. The best wool came from wethers. By 1311 the Priory possessed 555 such sheep, the sale of wool accounting for 60 per cent of the Priory's cash income. Ewes were milked, and the milk's goodness locked up as cheese.

31 *Ancient brooch from Victoria Cave, Settle. Cave remains indicate that farming began almost 6,000 years ago.*

32 *Riding the Stang (from George Walker's* The Costume of Yorkshire, *1814). The stang [pole] would be ridden if, for example, a farmer was guilty of wife-beating.*

From the mid-14th century livestock was being traded for corn. Jervaulx had a horse-breeding farm at Horton, in North Ribblesdale. Elizabeth Raistrick, writing in *The Dalesman* about the lot of the north-country housewife after the 14th century, referred to the cruck houses that lingered on into the 17th and even the 18th centuries. She quoted an early description of a ploughman's home, which he shared with his oxen:

> … of one bay's breadth
> Whose thatched spars are furred with sluttish soote
> A whole inch thick, shining like Blackmoor's brows,
> Through smoke that down the headless barrel blows.
> At his bed's feete feeden his stalled teame,
> His wine beneath, his pullen oer the beam.

The Raistricks possessed an account for the construction of two such houses at Airton in Malhamdale, from the Compotus of Dereham Abbey (1454), which owned land in this township. Timber (crucks for the framework) and carriage cost 5s. 1d., the expenses for erecting them being 1s. A carpenter was paid 4d. for setting big stones under the feet of the crucks and 6d. went towards the cost of 'delving' (quarrying) and carrying. The fitting of low walls that prevented the crucks from spreading cost 4s. 6d. and 8s. was paid for the purchase and carrying of the 'thakke' (thatch). Finally, there was the cost of 'wattling' the upper part of the walls and thatching the roof, a matter of 18s. 4d. The grand total was 37s. 9d.

Craven took on its pastoral form in the first half of the 16th century. The area was considered unsuitable for arable farming. In 1672, with the abolition of tolls on livestock sent from Scotland into England, a droving trade flourished. Tolls had been imposed because the considerable number of beasts being exported via Carlisle was affecting the livelihood of Yorkshire graziers, who had asked for heavy duties to be charged against the Scots breeders. Their cattle, reared and fattened at considerably less expense than in England, were undercutting local cattle in price.

About 1774 farmers in Craven were undertaking experiments in land reclamation. It was at High Greenfield, about the headwaters of the Wharfe, that Arthur Young discovered the farmer had improved more than 200 acres. He reclaimed 'black moory land' by burning and liming it, sowing with turnips, then laying down to grass with rye grass, clover, hay seeds, etc. Sound walling, good grazing and some draining accompanied the process. At the time of Young's visit, the land carried 20 horses, 40 cows, 1,200 sheep and 300 young stock for summering that made use of the moorland pasture surrounding them.

Autumn saw a movement of cattle from the breeding areas in the Highlands. They were driven to the trysts at Falkirk, Crieff or Dumfries, thence (in many cases) to the sweet limestone country of Craven. Lowing herds left Wensleydale for Ribblehead on one of two routes, via Widdale or by way of Snaizeholme and the old Cam High Road and Cam Fell. In either case, the cattle reached a celebrated hostelry at Gearstones, where a fair of Scottish cattle took place regularly.

In 1792 the Hon. John Byng crossed Cam to *Gearstones*, an inn he described as 'the seat of misery, in a desert'. He arrived when a Scotch fair was being held on the heath. Unluckily for him, Scotch cattle and the drivers crowded the front of the inn. Buyers and sellers were inside the building, most of them in 'plaids, fillibegs (kilts) etc.'. Byng observed, 'The only custom of this hotel, or rather hovel, is derived from the grouse shooters or from two Scotch Fairs.' Near Ingleton, Byng saw 'vast droves of Scottish cattle passing to the south'. Other droves wended their steady way through North Ribblesdale to Settle. At Long Preston, Byng observed yet another 'Scotch Sale' in progress.

33   *Tithe Barn, Bolton Abbey, now used for the storage of estate equipment.*

Drove routes were mainly on high, undeveloped land. There might be forty beasts in a drove. Their progress was at a rate of between 14 and 16 miles a day, at the end of which the cattle might be turned into large fields known as stances. At north English fairs, graziers who owned or hired land bought cattle and fattened them for a season before selling them on. There was a particularly large gathering on Great Close, Malham Moor described by Thomas Hurtley, the Malham schoolmaster, as 'a prodigious field of enclosed land, being upwards of 732 Acres in one Pasture; a great part of which is a fine rich soil, and remarkable for making cattle both expeditiously and uncommonly fat …'. As a historian, Hurtley is unreliable and Lister of Malham Tarn House tampered with his manuscript when he arranged for publication. Hurtley mentions that an important grazier who rented Great Close was Mr Birtwhistle of Skipton, who was said to have visited the Highlands and Islands of Scotland in 1745 (at the height of Jacobite fervour) and to have dealt with 5,000 head of Scotch cattle at one time, giving the animals time to rest before announcing a fair at which they would be sold.

Thomas Pennant (1772) gave a further insight into cattle droving: 'Kilnsey-Scar, ascend and get into a hilly, less pleasing country. Overtake many droves of cattle and horses, which had been at grass the whole summer in the remotest part of Craven, where they were kept for nine shillings to forty per head, according to their size.' Metal shoes, designed for wear by cloven-hoofed beasts, were fitted to cattle for long journeys. The blacksmith at Grassington made ox shoes and nails, taking them to Threshfield, Long Preston and Skipton for fitting. He charged 8d. a beast. By 1786 a large number of Craven graziers were making the trip to the Scottish trysts and sending back great droves of cattle. The trade ended in the 19th century when new markets were established and it became possible to transport cattle – fresh and still lively – in railway wagons.

34 *Interior of a Craven farmhouse.*

35 *Friar's Head,
Winterburn, a
17th-century building
that has long served as a
farmhouse.*

W.H. Dawson, in his *History of Skipton*, quotes comments on agriculture in the 'Vale of Skipton' made by a Craven farmer in 1793 and published in *View of the Agriculture of the West Riding* (Robert Brown, 1799). The 'Craven farmer' had made no material alteration or improvement for the last century or more to note. 'In some parts of Craven, though not near Skipton, I understand that within the last forty years there was a considerable portion of land in tillage; the ploughing was then performed by four or six oxen, and one or two horses; and I am informed that mode of husbandry answered very well'. Craven was famous for its long-horned cattle, particularly oxen, 'but since the introduction of Scotch cattle and grazing into the country the long-horned breed and of course tillage have been neglected'.

The Earl of Thanet, the main proprietor of land in Skipton, did not want to see his fine land ploughed but the anonymous Craven farmer considered it would be an advantage to the area if 'a proper mixture of grazing and tillage could be introduced; for though the country is not and never will be populous while the present mode of husbandry and monopolizing farms prevails, yet corn is generally higher in Craven than in most parts of the kingdom, because so very little is produced. If you suggest to them that the uplands may be kept in tillage, the reply is that they are so much exposed to mists, and the situation is so cold, that corn, particularly wheat, cannot seed or ripen'. Besides which, 'the uplands are very useful to them upon their present plan, to prepare the lean cattle for the better pastures, which some say would be too rich for them in that state...' The favourite grazing stock in the district was the black Scotch cattle plus 'some sheep, but on the lowlands very few, and on the uplands and moors they are not very numerous'.

In 1793 a manservant was paid about ten guineas a year, 'with board and washing in his master's house; a woman about five guineas, with the same'. A day labourer in husbandry received about 2s. or 2s. 6d. per day and found his own victuals; about ten years before, the common price was 1s. or 1s. 2d. 'The advance was owing to the

36 *Plucking geese, Keasden, near Clapham. The geese are being prepared for the Christmas market.*

introduction of the cotton manufactory into a country so little populous.' A man was expected to work 'from six to six in summer and from eight to dark in winter'.

Rennie, Brown and Shiraff, in a survey of agriculture in the West Riding published in 1794, classified Yorkshire cattle under four different heads. One of them was the long-horned or Craven breed, either bred and fed in western parts of the West Riding (Skipton and Malham districts) or brought from the county of Lancashire. The longhorn was 'a hardy type, able to stand the wet and precarious climate'. Bred locally, the longhorns and shorthorns provided all the milch cows of the dairy farms and, in some cases, were suitable for drawing the plough.

Towards the end of the 18th century, when landowners and farmers were improving the native stock by selective breeding, there came into being the shorthorn type of cattle which was to be popular over a wide area of Yorkshire for about 150 years. Some of the early shorthorns exhibited the sort of fatness about which John Bailey wrote in *Agriculture in Durham* when describing the local ox: 'At five years old he was not only covered thick with fat ... but this whole carcass in a manner loaded with it, and was then thought to be so wonderful an animal, and so far exceeding whatever had been seen before, that he was purchased to be exhibited.' The same fate befell the Craven Heifer, the lifespan of which covered the period 1807-12.

The aforementioned animal, bred by the Rev. William Carr of Bolton Abbey in a thatched building behind the garden belonging to Bolton Hall, was sold to John Watkinson, of East Halton, for 200 guineas. Watkinson is mentioned on the Craven Muster Roll of 1803, his occupation being that of butcher. The Craven Heifer was not to be slain, however. Its potential as a curiosity led to the decision to put it on public exhibition. Watkinson also commissioned an engraving of the animal and dedicated the picture to 'the Most Noble William Spencer, Duke of Devonshire'.

The Craven Heifer, four years old in March 1811, was 'still in a growing and improving state'. She was 11ft 2in long from nose to rump, 5ft 2in high at the shoulder and 3ft 3in broad over the back in three different places. The girth in the middle of the body was 10ft 2in, the girth over the loin 9ft 11in and the girth of the foreleg below the knee 7in. When the beast was to be exhibited at the *Cock Inn*, Haymarket in London, its weight was 312 stone, allowing 8 lb to the stone. The Craven Heifer might not have been the largest of Craven's super-animals, but it was far and away the best known, thanks to a few innkeepers who named their houses after the 'monstrous beast' and to the directors of the Craven Bank, who gave an etching of the Heifer a place of honour on their banknotes.

The Tempest family of Broughton bred cattle methodically. In the year of the Craven Heifer's death, Sir Henry Vane Tempest, a member of the Durham branch of the family, initiated the idea of a Shorthorn Register (which finally appeared in 1822). As early as 1813, cattle shows being held at Skipton included classes for 'short-horned cattle'. Stephen Tempest was the first president. His son, Sir Charles Robert Tempest, was the first to preside over the Craven Agricultural Society, formed in 1855 'to promote the breeding of good stock, and to encourage improvements in agriculture'. Their stock was well documented. A bull from Broughton was sold to the Duke of Devonshire. Peach, bred in 1839, was the most celebrated of the Broughton heifers. She had a dead weight of 3,096 lb and won the first prize of £20, and gold and silver medals, for the best exhibit at Smithfield's Christmas Show in London in 1843.

Skipton's horse fair was held on 23 September, unless that day was a Sunday. The Court Leet in 1809 complained that the sheep pens placed 'upon the fronts' on Monday evening by the publicans for the Tuesday cattle fairs were a nuisance, and the fair day was changed to Monday. Frederick Montagu, in his *Gleanings in Craven*

37   *Tithe Barn, Wigglesworth, which was eventually gutted by fire. Drawing by Godfrey Wilson.*

38 *Owd Mick, cattle drover. He collected and drove stock from farm to auction mart.*

39 *Jackie Holme, blacksmith at Austwick. Almost every Craven village had a blacksmith.*

(1838), observed that the cattle were not cooped up, hugger-mugger, in by-lanes and alleys, but had 'open space and fair play'. In the 1870s local tradesmen were placing wooden frames across their shop windows to safeguard them against damage by cows' horns. Straw was laid on the floors of shops and banks. In 1887 a Keighley newspaper referred to the 'fortnightly squalor in the streets' and the cattle market was moved to Jerry Croft in 1906.

In the 19th century the cattle markets held in Skipton were the most important in Craven and provided dairy products for the West Riding's industrialised towns. Settle was another important marketing centre, to such an extent that other fairs went into a steady decline. It was not unusual for fairs to be held on saints' days. Giggleswick adopted St Gregory's Day (12 March) for its livestock fair, and animals for sale were massed on the main roads of this small village.

Unhappily for visitors attending the annual Speech Day at Giggleswick School, the fair fell on the same day, so people and livestock had to co-exist. S. Compston, an old boy of Giggleswick School, in a series of articles published in the *Manchester City News* (1923), noted that farmers intent on doing business arrived in shandries or carts. Their wives and daughters met with friends – and shopped at Settle. Cattle were placed in front of houses, leaving space in between for traffic. Compston's home was on Belle Hill, which led steeply into the village. On fair day 'the road soon became dirty and clarty'. Cattle reared on 'lonely hillside farms, where they led placid lives, accustomed to gentle treatment, especially from the female attendants, were nervous

40 *Drystone walling, Malhamdale. Judging by its solidity and width, this wall is extremely old.*

and restless, some with distended udders'. Visitors attending the event at Giggleswick School 'picked their way as best they could. Dainty shoes and dresses were liable to become soiled, especially the expanded skirts of ladies who had begun to adopt the style of frocks crinolined with horse-hair, starch or steel hoops. A shower or two of rain made matters worst.' Pattens (light wooden shoes standing on oval iron rings) kept dainty feet above the dirt. Little shops offered sweets or pies, small beer and pop, and the pubs did great business.

Giggleswick Fair declined and ceased, unable to compete with the regular markets and farms held at adjacent Settle, where there were pens for sheep, space for cattle and a variety of stalls.

Charlotte Brontë wrote, 'Think of the North, a lonely moor – silent, and still, and trackless lies ...' Until recent times, the moors and fells of the Craven Dales were busy, the resort of gamekeepers and shepherds. On big estates the gamekeeper ruled the tenant farmers during the grouse-nesting season, when

41 *Details of a drystone wall, which was basically two walls in one held together by 'throughs'.*

his permission was needed to venture on to the moor to attend to sheep. A Dales shepherd worked more by the calendar than the watch, there being regular annual jobs, but the weather ruled everything. On the Pennines this was rarely helpful, offering chilly springtimes, cloudy summers and long winters, with accompanying snow and ice.

Thomas Joy, one of the last of the Craven shepherds, who died in 1982, supervised the stock on 1,845 acres on Grassington Moor. The moor had a common boundary with Stean Moor and was thus part of a vast tract of upland lying between the rivers Wharfe and Nidd. In Joy's day, heather occurred over about half of the moor; elsewhere there was mosscrop, the sedge known as 'cotton grass' which in summer whitened the upland plateaux. Thomas used to cut peat as fuel, beginning as early as April, so as to take advantage of the drying winds. 'Peat doesn't dry so well in June.' The mosses, a bilious green from sphagnum, were a death trap to unwary sheep. Yet, in the moist places, those same sheep, early in the year, 'push their noses between the bent and eat the bottom piece, the mosscrop, which is white, tender and sweet'. Thomas explained that the plant, as it first showed itself, had a point that developed into a 'fuzzy yellow top' and, in due course, into the familiar blob of 'cotton'.

On Grassington Moor the hand of man is everywhere evident. Thomas knew where prehistoric circles were to be found. He was aware of over 150 meer-stones, that defined the territorial rights of lead miners, and said that Duke's Quarry, at the moor bottom, yielded stone for the construction of the Town Hall at Grassington. A lead-smelting mill operated nearby for about 150 years. The moor had to be evenly grazed. When, as happened, Thomas reached the edge of it to find up to 700 sheep congregating on the low ground, he drove them higher; they might stay about an hour and then creep back again. Lambing sheep were taken from the moor in spring and the ewes, with their new lambs, were returned in the middle of May.

Just before shearing-time came the annual sheep-washing. A beck was dammed with stones and sods to create a pool. Around a thousand sheep were gathered and driven to a fold from which each animal was manhandled to the pool. Two men took

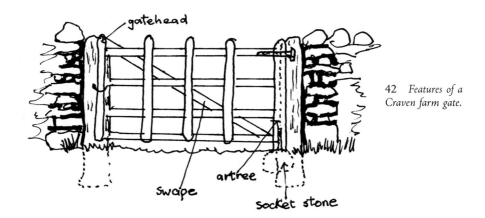

42   Features of a Craven farm gate.

43   *Thomas Joy, shepherd, Grassington Moor. Local farmers paid him for his duties.*

one sheep, one grabbing the breast, the other the buttocks. They deftly turned the animal upside down before tossing it into the water, from which it swam as best it could. True washing, or 'dollying', was a feature of past days, when a serious attempt was made to wash the underparts of each sheep. Another gather was for 'spaining', the separation of the lambs from the ewes, and the last gather was at the end of October when ewes were put to the tups, staying in the lower pastures until the beginning of December when they were driven back to the moor.

Moughton, Oxenber and Long Scar (Ingleborough) have long been stinted for stock-grazing, a stint representing the pasturage of a sheep. Every February, the farmers holding stints or gaits gathered round a cheery fire in the Parish Hall at Austwick to discuss mutual problems at the 'herd-letting', one of the oldest surviving customs in the Craven sheep country. On hills with much outcropping rock, the term acre meant little to the farmers. The grazing was assessed at an acceptable rate for the herbage. Four sheep gaits equalled one cow stint and eight gaits were needed for a horse to be kept. Normally only sheep were grazed. There are 579 gaits on Long Scar, 568 on Moughton and 120 on Oxenber Pasture. Apart from the big sheep pastures, there was the letting of the Little Wood, on Oxenber.

44 *Washing sheep at Keasden, near Clapham. This took place shortly before the sheep were shorn.*

45 *Collie dog on sentry duty before the introduction of cattle-grids.*

Herd-letting was, in fact, 'shepherd letting'. Before the Second World War farmers had little difficulty in finding shepherds for the stinted pastures, but a decline in official shepherding took place in the 1940s. C. Constantine received 1s. 10d. a gait for shepherding on Oxenber; T.J. Ward was the last shepherd on Moughton, paid 1s. 9d. a gait in 1945. Since 1947, when Harry Ballard was the last shepherd on Long Scar, paid 1s. 11d. a gait, shepherds have been hard to come by. The farmers grew resigned to doing the job themselves and appointed two men to care for the drystone walls that pattern the hills.

At the herd-letting the farmer appointed chairman-secretary kept the minutes – details of argument and decision – in an ancient calf-bound book, the first entry, in exquisite copperplate writing, being made early in the 19th century. By the 1940s the scribbled entries are in ballpoint pens. Austwick Moss, a stretch of original marshland, was divided up into 'dales' – thirty strips of land, allocated to neighbouring farms – where peat was cut as fuel.

Skipton was the major trading place for Craven's farm stock. It was also the setting for hiring fairs, notably the haytime gatherings attended by Irishmen, mainly from County Mayo in the far west, offering their services as haytime help. They were employed for a month, at a fixed sum of money which rose steadily from a low of about £5, this bargain including their keep. If haytime was wet they were set to work on such jobs as lime-washing the inside of shippons (a process known as 'bug-blinding'). The seasonal migration of Irishmen, which peaked just before

46   *Frank Campbell (left) with son and Dales-bred sheep, Craven's own special breed.*

the First World War but continued until about the 1950s, involved men from large families on small farmsteads. The man would leave home, with any large sons, about 9 May, his wife remaining to attend to the farm. Travelling to northern England by rail and boat, he was inclined to regard haytime as a holiday. Craven farmers hired good workers and, especially, good scythesmen.

One of the last of the migrant labourers the author heard about during research into the subject found work in 1957, when he was in his mid-fifties. He and his wife had 13 children, including nine sons, some of whom were able to accompany him to Craven. He missed the hirings at Bentham so travelled to Skipton and took work on a farm in Upper Wharfedale. With his haytime month served, he travelled eastwards to help with the corn harvest, and continued to Goole to help harvest potatoes and sugar beet.

Large numbers of cattle and sheep pass through a new auction mart at the outskirts of Skipton. In the old mart the black and white Friesian from the Low Countries supplanted the gentle shorthorn. Subsequently, several French-type breeds were introduced, trade at the new mart subtly reflecting changing fashion in farm stock. Across the Craven Dales, lowland fields that once sported a rich variety of wild flowers have, by ploughing and re-seeding with productive grass strains, changed the appearance of the district to a uniform green. Tractors do what used to be horse-work and the grandson of a farmer who walked round his land, dog at heel, kenning sheep, now rides on an all-terrain vehicle, light alloy crook beside him and the dog as pillion passenger.

Chapter 4

Natural Curiosities

In 1769 Thomas Gray hurried through North Craven after an extensive tour of the Lake District. He had time only to notice that 'Ingleton is a pretty village, situated very high, and yet in a valley at the foot of that huge monster of nature, Ingleborough.' Two torrents crossed the village, 'with great stones rolled along their beds instead of water, and over it are flung two handsome arches'. Thomas Pennant, antiquarian and naturalist, was in these parts four years later. He saw Ingleborough but 'had not the leisure to visit it'. He was given an account of its 'immense caverns' and the 'various plants very rare in other places'.

William Bray, energetic tourist in Derbyshire and Yorkshire in 1777, heard of the caves but remained on the surface. A second edition of his *Sketch*, published in 1783, was sketchy with regard to caves. Bray relied heavily on an account by John

47 *Early cave explorer. Visiting the North Craven caves began in the Romantic Age (1760-1820).*

Hutton, a Kendal clergyman, who had identified about twenty subterranean systems and had actually explored and described some of them. Hutton's book was first published in 1780 as an appendix to *Guide to the Lakes*, the cave section being reprinted a year later along with a dialect glossary of Craven. Bray also culled notes from an article in the *Gentleman's Magazine* (1761). The Ingleton show caves received national publicity, and visiting their gloomy recesses with a guide who carried a lanthorn became a spine-tingling prelude for 'gentlemen of taste and leisure' – and for some women – to visiting the awesome grandeur of the English Lake District.

The literary mind had been attuned to the idea of caving. Dozens of writers, including Milton, kept the cave as a special feature of the scene within which they could express themselves. The Craven caves – deep, dark, mysterious – were romanticised in the tourist mind by tales of boggarts, trolls and even fairies inhabiting the underworld. John Hutton, a cultured man who was familiar with classical writings, interjected into his prose verses from Virgil, Ovid, Addison and Milton. Although some of his arguments are sadly out of line with facts established later, he guessed rightly at the marine origin of the limestone which, he wrote, had once been 'in a soft pulpy state, approaching nearly to fluidity'. He had noticed the grey rock was made of 'the shells and other parts of fish'.

Two or three caves became tourist hotspots. Hutton was taken to Yordas Cave, in Kingsdale, a relatively short system with a yawning mouth and an ante-chamber that became known as The Chapter House. His guide, hired at Thornton-in-Lonsdale, was equipped with 'candles, lanthorn, tinderbox, etc'. A showman, he enthused about the effect the discharging of a gun would have in the confined space. Fortunately for Hutton, no one had a gun. Eighteenth-century visitors had already defaced the cave, removing 'pendant petrified works (calcite formations) which had been some ages in forming', setting them up as garden ornaments.

Weathercote Cave, in neighbouring Chapel-le-Dale, was to Hutton 'the most surprising natural curiosity of the kind in the island of Great Britain'. This deep rift was entered on a slippery path that culminated in a natural rock arch framing a fabulous 77ft waterfall appearing from behind a wedged boulder that Hutton called Mahomet's Coffin and compared with 'the coffin of Mahomet at Medina'. Hutton, by his pioneer researches, provided a quarry of fact and fancy which successive tourists did not hesitate to excavate.

William Wilson, an old soldier, was one of the guides who met tourists at Ingleton. John Houseman, topographer, described him in 1800 as 'a proper guide ... furnished with the necessary apparatus of a lanthorn, long candlestick, &c, for the purpose ... An account of his own adventures fills up the vacant intervals of time'. At Yordas, Wilson stands on

A

T   O   U   R

TO THE

C   A   V   E   S.

SIR,

ACCORDING to promife, I fit down to give you an account of our fummer's excurfion.—After having made the tour of the lakes, we were induced to proceed from *Kendal* by *Kirkby-Lonfdale*, *Ingleton*, *Chapel in the dale*, *Horton*, and *Settle*, in order to fee the caves and other natural curiofities in thofe parts of the *Weft-riding* of *Yorkfhire*. I muft own this fecond part of my tour pleafed me more than the firft, being peculiarly adapted to my tafte for natural hiftory, as alfo for the extraordinary and terrible. Some may be as much entertained with the profound, as others with the lofty; and fome may be as much amufed with the fublime, as others with the beautiful. This was the humour of my
B   genius,

48   *Introduction to Hutton's Tour. The Kendal clergyman explored a score or more of underground systems.*

49   *Dovecote Gill Cave, as portrayed by William Westall in 1817.*

50   *Yordas Cave, Kingsdale. Shortly after Westall completed his picture, debris from a violent storm virtually closed the cave mouth.*

a fragment of the rock and strikes up his lights, consisting of six or eight candles, put into as many holes of a stick; with each, by the help of a long pole fixed therein, he could illuminate a considerable space. His tobacco-pipe, being prepared and lighted, is held in his mouth; with his flambeau in one hand, and a staff in the other ... he gives us the signal of a march by 'Now come along'.

Wilson and 'his collection of luminaries' fell into the water flowing across the cave. He embraced again the earth while leading his party out of Weathercote Cave. Sliding down, he 'almost reached the margin of the black abyss before he could recover himself'. The party completed their ascent to the surface on hands and knees.

In 1808 the artist J.M.W. Turner made sketches for a painting of Weathercote Cave, including the vivid rainbow created in the spray when a shaft of sunlight, striking downwards into the void, illuminates it for a brief time in midsummer. John Ruskin, who 'discovered' Turner, was to write of Weathercote, 'It is the rottenest, deadliest, loneliest, horriblest place I ever saw in my life.' William Westall, engraver, who visited the show caves in 1817, produced 12 pictures, seven of them featuring Yordas and Weathercote. At Gatekirk, 'about half a mile above Weathercote, in the same valley',

51 *Professional guide to Yordas, 1817. He was equipped with a lanthorn.*

52 *Weathercote Cave, Chapel-le-Dale (Westall, 1817). The perched boulder became known as Mahomet's Coffin.*

he was impressed by the display of stalactites. They were 'hanging like large icicles from the roof; some that are just forming will crumble between the fingers; others are hard, though somewhat porous, with the inside composed of small crystals: the larger ones are as hard as marble and will take a fine polish.'

G. Nicholson of Malton, who in 1822 published his impressions of Weathercote and adjacent Hurtle Pot in a collection of *Six Views of Picturesque Scenery in Yorkshire*, described the prints as being 'drawn from Nature and on stone'. They are softer, more atmospheric, than the work of Westall while lacking Westall's fine draughtsmanship. With their hoops and voluminous skirts, women bravely walked along the paths to the show caves and stood at the brim of potholes. Among them was Priscilla Wakefield, gathering material for part of her *Family Tour through the British Empire* (the 13th edition of which was published in 1829). Priscilla wrote, 'The sides of the mountains in this part of the country are full of caverns, chasms and deep openings, of all sizes and shapes. Many of them are called pots, from being open at the top like saucepans, and most of these have their bottoms filled with water, from some stream that runs through the bowel of the mountain.' Moving cautiously down a

53   *Lithograph of Weathercote Cave. The waterfall was approached down a flight of steps and under a natural rock arch.*

clayey slope to the edge of the pool in Hurtle Pot, she was 'near losing my life, from a deception of sight caused by the shining of the sun from above on the surface of the deep, black water'. The mirror-like surface was broken when a large black trout surfaced. 'Swarms' of such fish were said to live in the subterranean pools. Eventually, in the interests of safety, Hurtle Pot was provided with a handrail and threepence was charged for admission.

The first true cavers in Craven on whom we have reliable information were John Birkbeck, of Settle, who was born in 1817, and William Metcalfe of Weathercote House, who was eight years younger. The caving era began in 1837 under the auspices of the Farrer family of Ingleborough Hall, Clapham. They owned a major part of

Ingleborough, the limestone in which is honeycombed with potholes and caves. In September 1817 Clapham Cave, at the head of Clapdale, was extended in dramatic circumstances. The mouth of the cave, a broad, deep gash at the base of a 100ft limestone cliff, had been known for years and explored for 56 yards. It was now decided to demolish a thick stalagmite barrier at the back of the cave. This action released a torrent and exposed a natural passage along which men, with lighted candles, waded and tramped for half a mile.

John Birkbeck, a member of the party, later teamed with William Metcalfe to explore the yawning shaft of Gaping Gill, 340 feet from rim to pebbly bottom. Their efforts were thwarted but they were the first to look into a chamber that seemed to be of cathedral-size. Edward Alfred Martel, a French speleologist using rope and rope ladder, claimed the honour of first descent into the main chamber in the summer of 1895. Before leaving the district he wrote a modest note in the visitors' book of the *New Inn* at Clapham: 'On Thursday, 1st of August, I went down Gaper Gill hole, &c.' Edward Calvert, the first Englishman to descend, was a member of the Yorkshire Ramblers' Club which, in a caving frenzy, explored other major potholes.

The caves of Wharfedale also had their visitors, especially Dow Cave near Kettlewell. In the tributary valley, Littondale, the main attraction was Scoska Cave. Show caves exist at White Scar (Chapel-le-Dale), Ingleborough Cave and Stump Cross, on Greenhow Hill.

54 *Martel making the first descent of Gaping Gill's main shaft in 1895.*

Paintings of Bolton Abbey by such masters as Cotman and Turner were exhibited in London, and drew attention to the sublime landscape in this part of Wharfedale. The Bolton Abbey estate of the Cliffords had passed to the Boyles through marriage in 1635. In 1748, Boyle married Cavendish, the 4th Duke of Devonshire. When William Carr, incumbent of Bolton Abbey from 1789 to 1843, persuaded the 6th Duke to open up some of his estate grounds to the public, 28 miles of footpath were made available to the public. A carriageway followed a riverside course to the Strid, where the mighty Wharfe surges through a narrow channel between banks of dark gritstone. William Wordsworth, commending the efforts of his friend Carr, wrote that he had 'most skilfully opened out its features; and, in whatever he has added, has done justice to the place by working with an invisible hand of art in the very spirit of nature.' Towards the end of his career, Carr was paid £100 for superintending the estate Pleasure Grounds. Given his other income, as perpetual curate, Master of the Boyle School and, in 1842, the second largest agricultural tenant at Bolton Abbey, many might envy the size of his incomings.

The Strid, key feature of walks in Bolton Woods, is said to derive its name from *stryth*, a tumultuous rush of water. The Wharfe is a 'flashy' river, rising and falling quickly as it responds to updale storms. At the Strid, a notch cut in rock 15 feet above normal water level, marks the height attained by the worst flood on record, which occurred in 1936. For a quarter of a mile the river, in the early manhood of its age, boils and bubbles. In the beginning the water eroded a series of potholes,

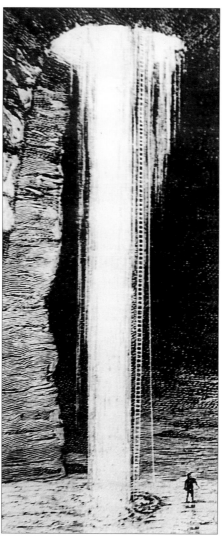

and further erosion led to the formation of the channel across which the foolhardy used to leap. It takes a confident man – or a fool – to perform the deed. The rocks slope awkwardly and they are mossy, offering little adhesion. Thomas Ryder (1867-1950), a spare-time photographer, pictured a large crowd of people at the Strid in 1906. He described the flanking rocks as 'not merely waterworn; they are footworn. The tread year by year of innumerable visitors has polished the great blocks until they are as smooth on their upper surface as stepping stones.' He photographed a jump for a lantern slide show.

A legend concerning the Boy of Egremont, one of the de Romilles, and dating from the mid-12th century, endures, having been romanticised by many writers, notably Wordsworth. At the Strid the Boy leapt the void but his favourite hound, which was on a leash, held back. Restrained, the Boy fell into the swirling water and drowned. In 1155 his grieving mother, Alice de Romille, anxious that her son's memory should be perpetuated, arranged for Augustinian canons to re-establish their priory from Embsay in a sheltered spot at Bolton, where the Wharfe had lost some of its turbulence. Historians point out that the Boy of Egremont was a witness when the Priory

55   Martel at the end of his epic descent of the main shaft at Gaping Gill.

56 *The Strid, Wharfedale, where the river gushes through a narrow channel between gritstone rocks.*

was actually founded, but Wordsworth, who knew this part of Wharfedale well, did not let facts spoil a good story. He gave credence to the legend with his poem *The Force of Prayer; or The Founding of Bolton Priory.* Of the Strid he wrote:

That fearful chasm,
How tempting to bestride!
For lordly Wharfe is there pent in
With rocks on either side.

The Rev. Thomas Parkinson claimed that when a person is due to be drowned in the Strid a white horse with a foaming mane rises from the water. J.H. Dixon, in his *Chronicles and Stories of the Craven Dales*, wondered if the White Horse of the Strid were connected with Sliepner, the steed of Odin whose mission was to convey the spirits of the drowned to the halls of Valhalla. Or whether there might be a connection with the White Horse of the Apocalyptic vision. Charles Kingsley, the cleric-author, having leapt across the Strid, boasted of the feat to his wife and children. Rudyard Kipling, who had family associations with Skipton, the grave of his grandfather being there, was aware of the Strid. In his story 'Pig', in *Plain Tales from the Hills*, he wrote, 'Now a Dalesman from beyond Skipton will forgive an injury when the Strid lets a man live; but a South Devon man is as soft as a Dartmoor bog.'

In 1894 Christopher Bailey, of Keighley, made a ladder descent into the Strid and reported seeing tree trunks, bleached almost white, jammed on the underside of rock ledges. Fifty years ago Richard Corin, dressed in a watertight rubber diving suit and roped to a back-up team on the bank, found that water at the entry point was 31 feet deep. The current was strong on the surface but sufficiently slack near the bottom to enable him to 'fin' upstream without help from the rope handlers. Within 50 feet of the lower end the current was too fierce for unaided swimming so a ropeman hauled him forward. Depths varied from 15 to 30 feet. The bottom of the river was littered with huge whitened limestone boulders. Three grapnels were recovered, offering grim evidence of past tragedies and indicating that dragging by grapnels along a littered riverbed was not practicable.

57   *Malham Cove lithograph. The limestone cliff is an exposure of the Mid-Craven geological fault.*

Frederick Montagu, in a reference to the viewpoints along the drives in 1838, gives the names of some of the seats: 'Oak, Clifford, Strid, Boyle, Ford and Devonshire.' Halliwell Sutcliffe broke into a sequence of romantic novels to pen what purported to be a non-fictional account of Dales life and traditions in 1929. With the stirring title of *The Striding Dales*, the book is still enjoyed by the romantically inclined reader. He captioned Reginald Smith's fine drawing of the Strid, in its setting of rock and woodland, 'Where Wharfe's full-bosomed stream narrows and frets between deep walls of rock.' Elsewhere, 'to stand where Wharfe narrows to the Strid is to be in woodland glamour, soft as a midsummer dream.' It is not enough for Sutcliffe that a White Horse should arise from the water; his White Horse 'comes from the racing flood, a warning of disaster to him who sees it'.

In the 1930s, when Ella Pontefract and Marie Hartley compiled books about Swaledale, Wensleydale and Wharfedale, they worked on Wharfedale when, in the dawn of the age of cars and buses, two men with horse wagonettes still waited for custom, and they drove along the carriage road that runs to the Strid, where cars were not allowed to go. The two ladies found their driver waiting at the Cavendish Pavilion, 'a café with a continental air in the woods'. The driver recalled when 'fifty-six of us there used to be drivin' this road and now there's only me and 'im [the driver of the other wagonette]'. Ella was told that several times he had brought a party to the Strid and gone back with one short: 'he seemed to feel the futility of it.'

Long gone are the days when drivers paid sixpence a day for using the carriage road, a figure that was doubled after the First World War. The Dukes of Devonshire owned the estate until 1926, when the Chatsworth Estates Company was formed. It is now the property of the Trustees of the Chatsworth Settlement, set up on the death of the 10th Duke in 1950.

Tucked out of sight at the head of Malhamdale are two mighty bastions of the limestone belt, the Cove and Gordale Scar. Some visitors to Malham Cove walked from Settle via Pikedaw to see where a beck (soon to become the River Aire) bubbled into view from the base of a vast curved limestone cliff, one of several majestic features of the Mid-Craven Fault. The cliff was buried in rocks that have since been eroded by water, thereby creating the Cove's imposing bow shape. After the last Ice Age, the water flowed from a swollen Malham Tarn over still-frozen ground to leap from the cliff, slowly cutting back the rock. Hurtley, the 18th-century schoolmaster at Malham, described as a 'rugg' a spell of rainy and tempestuous weather of the type to make 'a

more grand and magnificent cascade than imagination can form an idea of'. By the 19th century the waterfall was rarely seen. When it did appear there was so little water it dissipated in a cloud of spray.

Dark streaks on the limestone are formed from mosses and lichen that have absorbed airborne pollution, some of it traceable to industrial Leeds. Charles Kingsley, a keen angler who stayed at Malham Tarn House as the guest of Walter Morrison, was asked about the marks on Malham Cove. He thought for a moment, then explained they had been made when a little chimney sweep, escaping from his wicked master, tumbled off the Cove and left behind soot that had impregnated his clothing. The idea was incorporated in his classic story *The Water Babies*. Kingsley described the Cove as 'the awful cliff filling up the valley with a sheer cross wall'. He had seen the Aire emerging from its foot, 'coming up, clear as crystal, from unknown abysses', although what he actually saw was Malham Beck; the Aire is formed by a merging of two becks half a mile below the village.

Early visitors to Malhamdale were content to stand and stare at the Cove. To

58 *Gordale Scar, Malhamdale. Overhanging rocks tower to over 400 feet.*

William Bray (1777) it had 'something of the form of an amphitheatre, almost plain, but it has two or three ledges, like galleries, along the face of it, wide enough for one who has a strong head to walk with safety'. To the historian Thomas Dunham Whitaker (1805), 'it was stretched in the shape of a segment of a large circle across the whole valley'. Walter White (1861) described the Cove as 'pale, like marble, broken only by a narrow shelf – a stripe of green – accessible to goats and adventurous boys'.

John Ruskin (1879) was impressed by the softness. 'In Malham Cove, the stones of the brook were softer with moss than any silken pillow; the crowded oxalis-leaves yielded to the pressure of the hand and were not felt; the cloven leaves of the herb-robert … overflowed every rent in the rude crags with living balm.' What lay behind the bland face of Malham Cove fascinated the Rev. Charles L. Tweedale, of Weston in Wharfedale. He had a fervent but mistaken belief in the notion of a hollow cove. Claiming the spirits had informed him about it, he became known at Malham as the 'spooky parson'. There was a small cave system which has only recently been explored by cavers wearing wet-suits and having an independent oxygen supply. For much of the way, water filled the system to the roof. If anything had gone wrong with the caver's equipment there would have been no speedy way of rescuing him.

A second natural wonder of Malhamdale is Gordale Scar, which is vast and grey, with cliffs that overhang grandly at the top. A stream, the Gordalebec of the early 13th century, flows in a long, deep gorge set in a plateau of limestone and cut by rapidly flowing meltwater at the end of the Ice Age. Charged with lime, the water splashed against mosses and other vegetation, fixing them permanently as tufa, which is often fissured, like the trunks of ancient trees, and consists of layers each little more than one hundredth of an inch thick.

Water still flows down this awesome ravine. To those standing on the floor of Gordale Scar it seems to appear through an eyehole in rock. The name Gordale is derived from *gore* or *geir*, the ancient name for an angular piece of land. It has brought out the best in artists and the worst in writers. In the Romantic Age,

59 *Ebbing and Flowing Well, Giggleswick Scar. The effect is believed to be caused by a double siphon in the cliff.*

accounts usually included a reference to goats, which fascinated the 18th-century commentator, John Hutton, who we last met in the show caves of the Ingleton district. The animals 'frisked about with seeming wanton carelessness on the brink of this dreadful precipice, where none of us would have stood for all the pleasant vales washed by the Aire'.

Thomas Gray had a local guide, whose services did not impress him. Gray remained at Gordale for about a quarter of an hour. The cliff, he recalled, 'slopes forward over you in one black or solid mass without any crevice in its surface and overshadows half the area below its dreadful canopy: loose stones hang in the air and threaten visibly some idle spectator with instant destruction.' Then

60   *William Worthington presided for many years over Ingleton Glens, the local scenery company.*

it was back to the goats: he watched one dance, and scratch an eye with its right foot, in a place where he would not have stood stock-still.

Gordale Scar is mentioned in *The Water Babies*. Kingsley renamed it 'Lewthwaite Crag'. William and Dorothy Wordsworth were here on the last day of June 1807. They stayed for an hour, resting under 'the huge rock' and drinking of its cold waters, before ascending the side of the waterfall into Gordale's upper storey. William wrote:

> Gordale chasm, terrific as the lair
> Where the young lions couch.

The Romantics compared Gordale with the sacred fountain of Castalia on Mount Parnassus. Bishop Pococke declared that during the whole of his wanderings in Syria and the East he never met with anything so sublimely impressive. Victorian ladies climbed beside the waterfall 'at the risk perhaps of a little wetting by the ascending spray'.

A study of Gordale Scar, painted by James Ward (1769-1859) for Lord Ribblesdale in 1811, is a spectacular work in the Tate Gallery. The artist, son of a Cockney greengrocer, stayed at his lordship's home, Gisburne Park. He was more concerned about Gordale's psychological impact on the viewer than on plain topography, his contemporaries having pronounced Gordale 'unpaintable'. He responded to the challenge and, being the greatest animal painter of his generation, set a profusion of animals – deer and white cattle – in the foreground. They accentuate the scale of the place. The original canvas, which measured 14ft wide by 11ft high, did not appeal to Lord Ribblesdale and was tucked out of sight for years. Of modern artists, John Piper has provided a memorable impression. He conveyed the forbidding aspect of the Scar in a study dominated by purple, gold and buff.

In the late 1950s 'artificial' rock climbing began, the 'artificial' aspect being the so-called hardware, pitons and the like, which was used to ascend the smooth grey rock. It was said that if a climber had not completed his climb when darkness came, he hung from the rock face with great faith in his tackle, cat-napping until dawn. The climb was then resumed.

Not far from Gordale, and a feature on the same beck, is Janet's Foss, a waterfall given a fan-like appearance by a build-up of tufa, which Adam Walker (1779) referred to as porous petrifactions, 'crumbly when dry, and pulpy when wet, and shaped a good deal like crooked knotty wood'. The waterfall lies in a wooded ravine. The Janet of the title, Queen of the Fairies, was said to live in a cave behind the waterfall.

Giggleswick Scar, a western outlier of the limestone country, was on the busy Keighley-Kendal turnpike. Those who used the road passed a well which had the distinction of periodically 'ebbing and flowing'. In 1840 two Americans visited Giggleswick, in North Ribblesdale, to discover the secret behind the remarkable well. Water from the Scar runs through a stone basin at the roadside and at times of moderate rainfall the water level mysteriously falls then rises. The well was first described in a treatise called *Polyolbion* by Michael Drayton, published about 1612. A correspondent of the *Gentleman's Magazine* in 1760 called it 'the capital curiosity of the country', though similar springs formerly existed at Tideswell in Derbyshire and near Torquay. Brayshaw and Robinson, in *A History of the Ancient Parish of Giggleswick* (1932), described the well as 'a very unpretentious affair'. To the casual observer it was 'nothing more than one of the ordinary roadside wells, frequently to be found in the neighbourhood, that have been erected for the use of the wayfarer and of passing horses and cattle'. A local man was not taken seriously when he said the effect was related to the tides in Morecambe Bay.

It is likely that a double siphon exists in the limestone scar. When the two American visitors hired workmen to take the well to pieces and then replace it, their tampering affected its performance. They were said to have replaced upside down an inscribed stone which provided a mystical explanation of the phenomenon, ascribing it to a miracle performed long ago by a priest who wanted to show an evil-doer the wickedness of his ways. Fortunately, the inscription was noted on a paper that eventually formed part of the Pig Yard Club archives at Settle: 'Ye water dyd run yn even course botte Prioure Richard Moone [of Bolton Priory] bie ye power from above dyd mak it to rise and to fall yn a most curious manner paie hys tithes and dyd forsake hys evylie waies.'

The Rev. George Brown of Settle walked to the well every day in 1899, sometimes arriving at 5 a.m. Each time he spent over an hour studying the conduct of it, and several times, chiefly in June, he saw the 'silver cord', caused by an air current passing through the water. The Rev. Theodore Brocklehurst, who was at Giggleswick for over three decades, saw the well operating only twice. A Harrogate man and his fiancée, who left his car on 22 September 1974 after waiting for a severe hail and rain storm to abate, saw the water level in the well gradually fall. Then water rushed in and the level rose at least eight inches so that within no more than thirty seconds it

61   *Thornton Force, Ingleton Glens. The water pours 45 feet from a horizontal lip of limestone.*

reached almost to the brim. It then stopped as quickly as it had begun and the level sank rapidly to no more than four to six inches deep, at which time the 'silver cord' became faintly visible. They waited for another fifteen minutes but the performance was not repeated.

In the early 1960s, scholars from Giggleswick School (who own Scar Wood) kept watch on the well. During a period of 18 months up to February it was seen ebbing and flowing on 28 occasions; on 11 visits it was not. The Giggleswick School observations show that the temperature of the well water is virtually unchanging. Throughout the observation period, which including a notoriously cold winter, it was never lower than 8.1°C nor higher than 9.0°C.

Ingleton, a small tourist centre when gentlefolk with means and leisure explored the caves, began to exert a major appeal when, in the 1840s, the Midland Railway brought a host of day-trippers from the industrial towns. They had heard about narrow, secretive glens scoured by many waterfalls. Visitors' lower jaws dropped in astonishment when they beheld Thornton Force, a torrent that leapt from the limestone rim of a cliff into a deep plunge-pool. Joseph Carr, a local man, wrote about the scenic attractions in local newspapers. When, in March 1885, an 'Improvement Company' was formed, Carr was elected chairman and secretary. Entry was gained to Swilla Bottom and paths were laid and bridges built over the Doe. A reporter from the *Leeds Mercury* made the 'scenery' known to a large readership and the public was first admitted on Good Friday, 11 April. Rail excursions were organised and during Whitsuntide Ingleton had so many visitors that the caterers ran out of food, some local people resorting to the previously unthinkable task of baking bread on a Sunday.

Local farmers owned the glen through which the Twiss flowed and an element of rivalry developed between the two groups. (Not until after the First World War would the rights on both rivers be secured.) An ordinary visitor paid threepence for entry. The Victorian enterprise was commented on enthusiastically by Harry Speight, topographer, in his *Tramps and Drives in the Craven Highlands* (1895): since the formation of the Improvement organisation, ten years before, 'the place has become extremely popular as a health and pleasure resort'.

There had also been a significant building boom. In 1893 the 'maximum inrush' was reached during the season and Ingleton, standing above 'the deep romantic glen formed by the Greta', was visited by an estimated 100,000 people. The main attraction was 'the most romantic four miles of glen and mountain scenery to be found in our broad-acred county'. Refreshments were available above the Pecca Falls and at the Twisleton Hall farm. The ticket-box where a visitor must 'stand and deliver' was in Broad Wood and somewhat spoiled by large hoardings. Adventurers entered a ravine where a path followed the shelving wooded bank 'and presently descends by means of a ladder into a narrow defile below'.

Beyond lay the delightful glades of Swilla Bottom, a feature being the Lovers' Seat ('where it is said much nonsense has been enacted'). The wondering walker saw Pecca Falls, a series of cascades. 'In a time of flood, the whole ravine is choked with foam and the thundering water seems to shake the very foundations on which you stand.' Beazley Falls, at the head of the second glen, offered the sight of water that 'forms a succession of spouts, leaps, rapids, strids and eddying pools'. Forty years later writers were still enthusing about the twin glens. William Riley, in *The Yorkshire Pennines*, noted that 'the twin glens with their twin rivers present a series of charming pictures … the short journey has many and varied fascinations – romantic ravines, pretty cascades, imposing waterfalls and a marvellous array of flowers'. (The glens were to be stripped of their floral wealth by grasping hands.)

Chapter 5

Packhorse Ways and Turnpike Roads

For over six centuries the prime form of transport in the Craven Dales was packhorse or pony, the era beginning in early monastic times and ending with the transport revolution in the early 19th century. Wool was transported from the granges to the abbeys and thence to the ports from which it was exported to the continent. The wool trade was pre-eminent and Fountains Abbey had over one million acres of land in Craven. A pony engaged in transporting wool was fitted with a wooden frame known as a 'crutch'. Other goods were borne using panniers or wooden saddles of various sizes. Horses or ponies returned with supplies for those engaged at the granges or in the monastic mines.

62   *Packhorse bridge, Stainforth, North Ribblesdale, which was donated to the National Trust in the 1930s. The composer Elgar's fondness for this bridge prompted local orchestral members to play some Elgarian strains.*

By the Dissolution, the district was overlaid with a network of packhorse ways – the 'green roads' of later times. In the absence of handy fords, simple but elegant bridges spanned becks, a fine example being that crossing the River Ribble at Stainforth (stony ford). Kendalman's, a well-used ford on the Ribble between Giggleswick and Settle, was presumably used by packhorses taking wool from Kendal to the West Riding towns. Some of the larger bridges were constructed of wood but in due course rebuilt in stone at the expense of a general levy on the county. An example is at the head of Thorns Gill, North Ribblesdale, where a commemorative stone indicates that the bridge was rebuilt at the expense of 'the whole West Riding'.

The main packhorse routes were in use long before the Enclosure Acts led to the district acquiring a pattern of drystone walls. A packhorse train was made up of between 20 and 40 horses or ponies and a popular animal was a jaeger, imported from Germany, so the man in charge of a packhorse train might be known as a 'jagger'. In the Craven Dales the Galloway from south-west Scotland was also favoured. Attending a packhorse train were a driver and several assistants. The harness of the leading pony was fitted with bells made of iron or brass signifying the leader of the team and giving warning of its presence, especially at the approach to narrow places like bridges.

A vast range of goods was transported along the packhorse ways, from hides to lead. Large baskets were used for charcoal and peat and smaller baskets for iron ore and coal. Packhorses conveyed to upper Wharfedale and Littondale roofing slates that had been quarried in Coverdale and lead was borne across the moors from many of the smaller mills to Grassington. A pony transporting lead ingots from mill to market was fitted with panniers suitable for two ingots, each weighing eight stone. Salt was borne from coastal pans to Craven villages and farms, being a vital necessity in the preservation of meat for winter consumption.

In 1776 thirty packhorses a week travelled between Settle and Kendal with wool, yarn and cloth. A greater number were employed between Settle, Skipton and the West Riding towns of Leeds and Halifax. Raistrick has recorded that the mines at

63 *Stone-breakers on the Road (from* The Costume of Yorkshire).

64   *Tollhouse, Keighley-Kendal turnpike, near Settle.*

Grassington sent their lead and silver from the smelt mills to Gargrave, Skipton and Leeds by packhorse train. On the return journey the animals were loaded with coal and stores. In Bastow Wood, Grassington were walled and turfed enclosures made during the 17th and early 18th centuries by miners who, in return for caring for the pack ponies, were allowed to enclose such small crofts for themselves and to cultivate the ground.

In the second half of the 17th century a movement began whereby private (usually local) enterprises obtained Acts to create turnpike roads. The cost of maintenance was to be met by contributions from road users, who were intercepted and charged at spiked tollgates. Work in the Craven Dales occurred mainly between the 1750s and the 1830s. In June 1751 an Act was obtained to turnpike the road from Lancaster to Richmond, from where a good road was to extend to Yarm, thus providing a reliable coast-to-coast highway.

The surveyor for the eastern division, which took in Cam Fell, was Alexander Fothergill. In 1795 a deviation from the original route avoided the long climb from Bainbridge in Wensleydale along the line of the Roman road to Gearstones. The turnpike now ran from Hawes up Widdale to the watershed at Newby Head and down to Gearstones, where it picked up the line of the Roman road through Chapel-le-Dale. West of Newby Head, milestones for the 'Lancaster & Richmond Road', made of cast iron and dating from about 1825, are still in evidence.

65 *German gypsies camping on Newby Moor, the open common between Clapham and Ingleton, 1907.*

The Skipton-Harrogate road was turnpiked in 1777. The line established is almost that of the modern A59, a busy trans-Pennine trunk road. The trust expired in 1876. An Act of 1753 concerning 'the road between Keighley in the Westriding of Yorkshire and Kirkby in Kendal in Westmorland' mentioned its narrowness in many places and the fact that it was ' very ruinous and in great decay and not only impassable for wheel-carriages, but very dangerous for travellers'. The Keighley-Kendal Turnpike Trust consisted of 40 'qualified gentlemen' who raised capital at 4½ per cent interest, to be used on the remaking of the road and recouped out of the tolls.

The first meeting of the trust took place at 'the dwellinghouse of Robert Johnson in Settle'. In the end, its work was carried out by relatively few members, most of them prominent landowners living in North Craven. It was confirmed that the width of the roadway was to be seven yards, of which five yards were to be maintained as a metalled track. A drawing of a tollgate shows a large padlocked gate and a smaller gate with a bolt operated from within the tollhouse. In 1762 the road between Keighley and Skipton, a distance of over nine miles, was ordered to be 'completed at 4s. a rood and to be kept in repair for £20 a year'.

The increase in traffic did not always keep pace with the cost of maintaining the roads and before long the trust had incurred a debt of over £30,000. Besides which, many travellers found the paying of consecutive tolls on a long road journey both costly and inconvenient and sought to by-pass the toll bars by taking to obscure lanes round them. Things went from bad to worse. There was difficulty with the bank, the rate of interest on the capital was reduced and the amount spent on the road fell almost to nothing. The final blow to the trusts came when Macadam, Telford and others brought new ideas to road building and surfacing.

Chapter 6

An Inland Waterway

The shape of Skipton was firmly set from 1773, when the canal arrived and barges delivered coal to the back doors of the mills. Canals became a craze with the investing public after 1761, when the Duke of Bridgewater's canal near Manchester was opened and its economic value realised. A major link between Skipton and the large industrial centres lower down the Aire valley was the 127-mile-long Leeds and Liverpool Canal. It sprang from an idea put forward by Joseph Longbottom and was to have as its motto *Ab ortu ad occasum* ('From the rising to the setting', or 'From East to West'). With navigable water extending eastwards from Leeds, the proposed canal would link the German Ocean, subsequently known as the North Sea, with the Irish Sea.

John Hustler, a Quaker wool merchant leading a group of Bradford businessmen, supported Longbottom's idea. Its proponents claimed it would reduce transport costs on the carriage of limestone from one shilling to one penny per ton per mile. Whitaker, in his *History of Craven* (1805), was not reconciled to the Industrial Revolution but conceded that a canal would be desirable. He noted that 'a single horse, which forty years since toiled from Knaresborough to Skipton with a sack of wheat upon its back, will now, with equal or greater ease, draw a boat upon the canal laden with forty tons of the same necessity of life.' Two Craven men closely associated with the early history of the venture were Mathew Wilson, of Eshton Hall, and Danson Roundell, of Gledstone Hall in West Craven.

A committee meeting at Skipton agreed to a petition for a private Bill in Parliament. It was strongly opposed by landowners who foresaw the ruin of several thousand acres of rich meadow, leaving insufficient hay for fodder for cattle. Nonetheless, the Act was passed in May 1770, with an authorised capital of £260,000 in £100 shares. Skipton was the venue of the first general meeting of the proprietors, held on 20 June, and the shares were taken up in a relatively short time. Peter Garforth of Skipton had the frustrating task of negotiating with landowners for the required strip of land, James Brindley was appointed as engineer, and the cutting of the canal from Bingley to Skipton began in 1771. A small army of navvies, many of them Irishmen, undertook the spadework. There being no requirement for locks, this section was completed in the spring of 1773.

On the opening day Skipton Brass Band boarded a barge and played cheerful music as it was hauled by horsepower all the way to Bingley. It had been arranged for the Bingley Band to do likewise, in the reverse direction, but when the musicians boarded their barge it promptly sank! The *Leeds Intelligencer* reported the otherwise joyful events at Skipton. Two boats laden with coal arrived and the coal was sold at half the normal price. 'The bells were set a-ringing ... there were also bonfires, illuminations and other demonstrations of joy.'

An extension of the canal to Holme Bridge, Gargrave was effected in the spring of 1773. By June of the following year, with the canal open from Esholt to Holme Bridge, 18 boats were trading mainly in coal and limestone. By 1777, with the navigable stretch open only from Leeds to Gargrave, and Engineer Brindley's estimate of £260,000 proving wildly over-optimistic, the money ran out. The prosperity of the 1760s had given way to recession, mainly as a consequence of the revolt of the North American colonies.

Financially restructured, the canal was completed in 1816. None of the original promoters lived to witness that happy day. Early account books of the company support the expectation that the main goods to be carried between Skipton and Bradford would be corn and lime. In the reverse direction, coal not limestone was the bulkiest and most profitable freight on the new canal (which, locally, had become known as 't'cut'). Coal, delivered to the back doors of local mills, transformed an industrial life that had been based on wool and Skipton evolved as a cotton town. A Craven farmer quoted by W.H. Dawson stated that 'the canal ... seems to have taught us the possibility of making tolerably level roads, even in a mountainous country; several excellent ones have been made within the last five years; the materials chiefly limestone, broken to about the size of an egg.'

Lord Thanet, of the Skipton Castle estate, had opposed the canal project, hoping through his quarrying to preserve his monopoly on the local limestone trade. Now he secured a private Act of Parliament to make a navigable cut to the canal 'from a place called the Spring, near Skipton Castle ... to join and communicate with the navigable canal from Leeds to Liverpool in a close called Hebble End'. His Lordship's intention was to develop his limestone quarry at Haw Bank. In 1785 that quarry was leased to the canal company. The proximity of quarry traffic to the Castle being a nuisance, in 1792 Lord Thanet – not unreasonably – refused permission to make a tramway through the Castle Yard to the Cut. The company, in response, extended the Springs Canal to meet a new tram-road from Haw Bank, a road that ended in a staithe a hundred feet above the canal.

The work of cutting through the solid rock on which the Castle stood was both expensive and dangerous. The parish registers for January 1796 record the death of Thomas Paley, 'killed by a blast of gunpowder behind the Castle'. Once the new scheme was operating, barges were damaged by limestone cascading from chutes set at a great height above the waterway. The noisy process also upset his Lordship and family in the Castle, and in 1835 an inclined tramway was introduced and quarry material tipped from the more modest height of about twenty feet above the barges.

66   *Skipton Rechabites on a canal boat trip, c.1920. The Leeds and Liverpool Canal winds its way through the Craven Lowlands.*

Among the canal projects that never left the drawing board was an idea, put forward in 1774, to link Settle with the Leeds and Liverpool Canal via a cut that would join it at Thornton-in-Craven. Four years later, another group of speculators proposed to dig a canal from a pond called Paley Puddle at Settle to link the town with Lancaster. A long tunnel would be required through the hill known as Huntworth. If this plan had been carried out, Ingleton would have featured on the canal map of the land. Robinson and Brayshaw, in their history of the ancient parish of Giggleswick, published in 1932, commented, 'Local investors did not bite, and no more was heard of the proposal.'

Chapter 7

The Iron Roads

S kipton was connected with the rail network in 1847. In that same year the Castle estate recorded its first sale of freehold property in the High Street – the site for the Craven Bank's new premises. As Geoffrey Rowley, local historian, was to reflect: 'The town was outliving its feudal past and becoming exposed to the outside world.' Even so, Major Cookson, writing in 1859, mentioned the refusal of the Tufton family, owners of the Castle estate, to make land available for long-term development: 'The town has no room to expand; the castle people will not sell the fields around it on any building terms.' The former Midland Railway served the district almost exclusively. In 1846 the Leeds and Bradford line had opened. The section from Shipley to Skipton, which was operating in 1847, became known as the Leeds and Bradford Extension Railway, a company leased by the Midland. At the same time, a branch line from Skipton to Colne connected with the East Lancashire Railway.

Skipton's first station was an imposing structure built by Sugden, Simpson & Clarke at a cost of £2,330. A writer in the *Craven Herald* in 1857 lamented the lack of covered waiting accommodation on the northbound platform. The *Leeds Mercury* of 1873 was concerned at the lack of a refreshment room. The single waiting room, about sixteen feet square, earmarked for male passengers, was a tiny space crowded on market days with cattle drovers (and sometimes their dogs) and by butchers. 'As the men are frequently "the worse for drink", the first and second class passengers are "left out in the cold"'.

The Little North Western Company opened a line from Skipton to Morecambe, and in 1850 the station at Clapham, which stood one and a half miles from the village, became a junction when tracks were laid to Ingleton. This was a frontier town in the sense that the Midland extended to one end of an enormous viaduct spanning the Greta gorge. Beyond was a London and North Western Railway branch to Lowgill, where it joined the Lancaster-Carlisle. Each company had its own station and engine shed for one engine. The Clapham-Lowgill route, by arrangement with its rival, shortened the Midland service to Scotland by almost 24 miles. But it was inconvenient and, at a time of vigorous inter-company rivalry, did not suit an up-and-coming Midland, which eventually constructed the now celebrated Settle-Carlisle line, a 72-mile long 'middle route' to Scotland. Opened for goods traffic in 1875, and for passenger trains in the following year, the Settle-Carlisle enhanced the

67   Skipton Old Railway Station, dating from the 1840s.

status of Skipton. The town prepared for the Midland Company's latest enterprise in 1876 by closing the old station and building its successor a little to the west. It was intended to impress the public. Cyril Harrington, an art teacher, was to describe it as a Gothic structure 'showing the 19th century in all its muddle-headed romanticism and middle-aged pomposity'.

The Settle-Carlisle was a first-class, all-weather route, making clever use of two north-south valleys – North Ribblesdale and the Vale of Eden. Perspiring firemen called a ruling gradient of 1 in 100 for the first 22 miles the Long Drag. The line reached its summit at Aisgill (1,169ft) and, even at times of exposure to harsh winter weather, became a lifeline for the folk living at small villages and remote farmsteads in a swathe of Craven that had been ill-connected to the outer world by narrow roads. An official guide to the Midland Railway (1880) described the route taken, in the homely phraseology of the engineer-in-chief, as a great whale lying on its belly, 'its nose at Settle and its tail at Carlisle. A steep ascent carries us up, a long incline carries us down.'

The most conspicuous features of the Settle-Carlisle are lofty viaducts spanning deep water-carved valleys known as gills. The most conspicuous viaduct, at Ribblehead, a meeting place of small valleys, is prosaically known as Bridge No. 66. At the time of its construction, in the 1870s, it was known locally as Batty Wife Viaduct, after a romantic legend associating it with the tragic death of a man and his wife in a flooded pot-hole that was filled in during the construction period. The viaduct is now widely known as Ribblehead, though the beck flowing from a cave near the road is merely a tributary of the great river. This enormous structure, one of the

68 *Skipton New Station in Victorian days. There was a flurry of activity when the Settle-Carlisle line, the middle route to Scotland, was opened to passenger traffic in 1876.*

69 *Skipton station on the day the Grassington branch line was opened in 1902.*

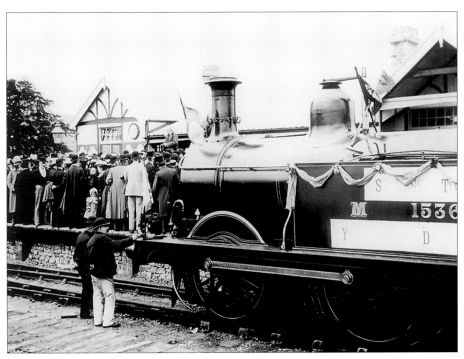

70 *Opening day of the Grassington line, 1902, a railway with a short life which faced competition from bus companies.*

wonders of Craven, has 23 piers (24 arches) and attains a maximum height of 105 feet. It is clamped at either end by steep embankments and has Whernside (2,414 feet) in the background.

Ribblehead viaduct was not built on wool, as many believed. The 30,000 cubic yards of masonry rest on beds of concrete laid on bedrock. The wool connection was probably to do with Bradford, then the wool capital of the world. It is not unlikely that the Midland Company, strapped for cash, borrowed from the woolmen. Job Hirst, a sub-contractor at Ribblehead, was a West Riding man who had been taught about making 'big bridges' in the county. Before arriving at Ribblehead with his sons he had experienced building a railway through difficult terrain in India. He died after being mugged while returning from a business trip to Ingleton, and his grave in the churchyard at St Leonard's, Chapel-le-Dale, is one of the few bearing inscriptions. Most of those who died at the railway shanty towns around Ribblehead – men, women and many children – were interred in unmarked plots. They have now been commemorated, outdoors, by an inscribed metal tablet set on an upstanding piece of local stone.

The hamlet of Hellifield became a busy village, presiding over an important rail junction when the Midland system was joined here by the Lancashire and Yorkshire Railway. A new station, built by the Midland Company, was brought into use in 1880. The stone for its construction came from Shipley, the dressings from Haworth

71 *Shanty life at Ribblehead, 1870s. Impression of a navvy hut. (Drawing by Betty Harrington.)*

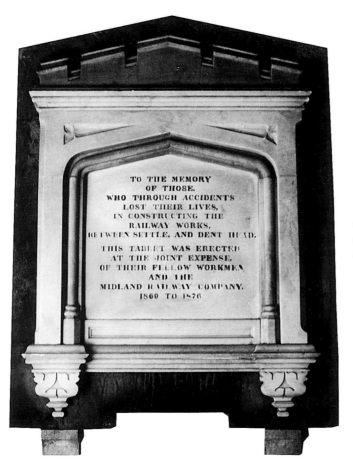

72 *Memorial to Settle-Carlisle railway workers, Chapel-le-Dale church.*

73 *Two Johnson 4-4-0s head a train at Hellifield in Midland days.*

and the flagstones for the platforms from Hawes in Wensleydale. A new road a quarter of a mile long linked the new station with the village. An auction mart was opened in 1887 and a large Temperance Hotel in 1890. With an influx of railway personnel, the population of Hellifield trebled in about twenty years and in 1931 totalled 1,026.

The last great railway project in Craven involved Grassington. What became known as the Yorkshire Dales Railway, after the name of the promoting company, received approval for a rail spur off the Skipton to Ilkley route that would connect Grassington with the railway system. Hopefully, it would become a commuter and tourist route, also boosting local industry. Walter Morrison MP, the 'Craven millionaire', cut the first sod in June 1900 and the line was operational rather more than two years later. Though known as the Grassington Line, the railway terminated at Threshfield, thus avoiding the construction of a viaduct across the steep-sided valley of the Wharfe.

On the Grassington side of the river was built a red-tiled terrace that became known locally as Boiled Egg Row, the implication being that it stood four minutes' walk from the station. This conjures up the pleasant picture of a businessman neatly dividing his life between the stone-and-mortar canyons of a great city and a pleasant village in the Dales. He alights at Threshfield, briefcase in hand, and sniffs the air, which is tingling fresh. Moving his bowler hat to the back of his head, he steps out jauntily. Our man of two worlds has the pleasant thought that when he has crossed the river bridge, his home, his family – and his boiled egg – are near at hand.

The railway came to Upper Wharfedale at a time of local industrial depression and there were empty homes for the newcomers to buy, which is one reason why few buildings of Victorian design are to be seen. The death knell of the Grassington

74   *Victorian iron canopy, Hellifield railway station.*

Railway was competition from the motor bus. The last train, with 54 passengers, ran on 21 September 1930. The line terminates at Swinden, near Cracoe, where there is a huge limestone quarry. Skipton's association with the railway reached its zenith at the dawn of the 20th century, when 507 men were employed. In 1923 the Midland Railway Company became the London, Midland and Scottish.

The line from Skipton to Ilkley closed in March 1965. A preserved stretch, from Embsay to Bolton Abbey, provides the joy of travelling by steam train to the visiting public. At Bolton Abbey, a new station building was constructed largely on traditional lines, preserving the flavour of the past.

When the line opened in 1888, an extra 40 trains ran on the first Bank Holiday, bringing trippers from as far as Liverpool, York and Doncaster. Horse wagonettes awaited the trains, ready to take day-trippers on a tour of the district. The Midland Railway was urged by one of the locals to avoid bringing too many trippers, who tended to pluck wild flowers and 'leave a lot of litter'. On one busy Bank Holiday, ten coaches hired by Thomas Cook were late, the rails at Skipton being congested. King George V, visiting Bolton Abbey for the grouse shooting, arrived by train and crowds lined the road from the station to the *Devonshire Hotel*. During the Second World War, a train bearing George VI on a tour of the north was stopped at Bolton Abbey, where an air-raid shelter had been excavated in banking. After the war, a local man used the shelter in lieu of a garden shed.

The lifting of tracks between Wennington, Lancaster and Morecambe in January 1966 meant that trains from Skipton and the West Riding were diverted via Carnforth. In February 1970 the Skipton to Colne line, via Barnoldswick, closed down and the trackbed was removed. The Settle-Carlisle was threatened with closure in 1989 but – against all odds – it thrives, with a busy mixture of passenger and goods trains, plus diversions of the most modern passenger stock on those Sundays when the Lancaster-Carlisle is closed for maintenance work.

Chapter 8

The Motoring Age

Some fifty years after the railways ended the isolation of much of the Craven Dale country, the first horse buses were raising the dust on the unmetalled country roads. Ezra Laycock, of Cowling, owned the first motor bus in the whole of Yorkshire. He and his eldest son Rennie, aged 15, journeyed from their remote little village to London, pounding the streets of the capital for three days and visiting Brighton without success. Laycock and Stephenson, his mechanically-minded partner, contacted Messrs Milnes-Daimler and Co. (not *the* Daimler of Coventry) and placed an order for one single-deck vehicle. The body was built in London and 18 folk, including of course the partners and their wives, travelled to London, collected the bus and drove it back. Messrs Laycock and Stephenson were soon running a regular service in the immediate district.

By 1930 the age of the bus was well established. Around 400 buses were leaving Skipton daily on regular runs to the surrounding areas and about 100 buses were passing through the town on long-distance routes. Arthur and Elizabeth Raistrick, in their site study, noted that 'the Market Place and High Street, almost any hour of the weekend, present a heart-breaking spectacle of congestion, noise and constant arrival and departure.' Men and women with individual manners operated early bus services. Mrs Lamb of Settle opened up a bus route between the Talbot Yard and Horton-in-Ribblesdale. The original 14-seater ended its career at Intake Brow, Helwith Bridge when, instead of braking on meeting another vehicle, a new driver touched the accelerator and the vehicle left the road. The roof fell off, the sides collapsed and the three passengers, thankfully unhurt, found themselves in the open air with rubble all around them.

The Simpson brothers, Arthur and Vic, who lived in Skipton, developed bus travel in Malhamdale for the benefit of local people, ramblers and youth hostellers using orange-painted Pioneer buses. The project began on Christmas Eve 1925, when they and their brother-in-law, Jim Windle, ran a 14-seater American-type bus from Skipton to Settle. No tickets were issued on that first run. The timetable was devised with Miss McKell, a schoolteacher, in mind. She lived at Gargrave and it was known that she had to be at school, further up the road, by 9 a.m. Starting a bus service in 1925 was uncomplicated, for no licence was needed. Petrol cost 7½d. per gallon if 200 gallons were ordered. Arthur Simpson, visiting Leyland Motors in Lancashire to

75 *Thornber family motoring near Pen-y-ghent.
The first car to pass through Skipton, in 1897,
belonged to Walter Morrison.*

acquire three new buses, was asked which colour he preferred for the bodywork. He arranged for Pennine buses to be painted orange, after the colour of the bus in the works yard that took the works football team to its matches.

By 1928 Pennine had competition from the Ribble service which, from a base in east Lancashire, had moved to Ingleton and Skipton. The Pennine response was to extend their service to Morecambe without lowering the fares. Sense prevailed when the two companies signed a joint agreement on the 50-50 pooling of mileage and money on the Lancaster and Malham routes. There were initially no official bus stops. A driver drew up wherever he saw an interested person and no potential customer was refused access. When, as happened occasionally, a 27-seater Lioness was packed, the conductor sat on a mudguard.

In straitened times, farmers were regular customers, many of them wearing clogs. The bus was occasionally used for transporting a calf swaddled in sacking and at Austwick I saw a passenger alight with a goat. Farmers' wives used the bus when going to market with butter for sale. They carried the butter in large baskets and, in summer, kept it cool by wrapping it in rhubarb leaves. It was not unusual for a person living at Hellifield or Long Preston to ask the driver to call at Dr Lovegrove's surgery at Settle to collect a prescription. The driver would do so, then go on to Shepherd and Walker's to have the prescription dispensed. A popular run for Settle folk on a sunny Sunday was to the top of Buckhaw Brow, where a Mr Robinson erected a stall and sold fruit, vegetables and rabbits.

The West Yorkshire Road Car opened a depot at Grassington in Upper Wharfedale. Code-named Service 71, the bus negotiated some 19 miles of narrow, hilly roadway, passing through Rylstone, Hetton and Cracoe before touching the Wharfe valley. It then traversed the austere upper valley to Buckden. The company had taken over the business of 'Kit' Chapman, who operated horse-drawn coaches in Wharfedale, handling the Royal Mail and light goods as well as passengers. The red-sided West Yorkshire buses carried children, office workers and quarrymen. From 1930 to 1935, the 6.25 p.m. bus from Grassington to Skipton had a mailbox clipped to the front. Anyone could flag down the bus and post letters, which were collected by the postal authorities when the bus arrived at Skipton. There was also a service from Grassington to Ilkley.

The Road Traffic Act took much of the fun out of buses. No longer could the operator accept calves in sacking, crates of hens and even piglets, which local farmers were inclined to hand over to the driver for delivery. The driver's reward might be a brace of rabbits or a pound of cheese or butter.

Skipton in the early 1920s was a calling place for intrepid Yorkshire motorists bound for resorts on the Lancashire coast or the Lake District and the town had complex traffic problems. Caroline Square was the crossing of a road connecting Leeds and Preston and another on its way from Keighley to Kendal. Two smaller roads, from Knaresborough and Grassington, added their quotas. The consequence was a lot of traffic in the High Street.

76 Skipton High Street, 1928, with a scattering of cars – and a bus.

77 Horse-assisted motor car on Park Rash, Kettlewell. The car had foundered during a trial.

Walter Morrison, of Malham Tarn, gave up horse transport and hired a Wolseley car from the *Golden Lion* inn at Settle to transport him on business or to meetings (he was a governor of Giggleswick School). He then invested in a Fiat, obtained for him from a Settle garageman and engineer called Billy Slinger. Being 'a big chap', Morrison needed a large car. He did not intend to drive the car himself, and so he sent his coachman, then aged 75, to Billy Slinger for lessons. Billy was apt to lose his patience when his pupil was not driving well and rebuked him by kicking his foot off the clutch. After the coachman changed to being a chauffeur, he travelled into town with horse-drawn trap and returned with the car, but this did not respond when he shouted 'whoa!' at the approach to the stable yard at Malham Tarn House, and the car grazed one of the walls at the gateway.

78   A.D. Simpson, one of the founders of the Pennine bus company.

At Settle, petrol was measured out from cans by Pratts, of Cammock Lane, and distributed by a Mr Mashiter using horses and lorry. The demand was not large and a garage might order 50 gallons at a time. The Model T Ford had a petrol tank situated under the seat, which meant that when the fuel supply was low the engine cut out.

79   Snowbound Pennine bus. The longest direct route was between Skipton and Morecambe.

DISTANCE FROM INGLETON:
CLAPHAM. 4 MILES.
KIRKBY LONSDALE. 6 MILES.

Barton's Garage
C BARTON PROPRIETOR
CLAPHAM · YORKSHIRE
(TELEPHONE 2)
KIRKBY LONSDALE · WESTMORLAND
TELEPHONE: 15

ECCLES TRAILER CARAVANS ON HIRE.

Agents and Repairers for Morris Cars.   Breakdown Outfit available at any hour.

Authorised Repairers to R.A.C. and A.A. (4 Star).   First-class repairs and overhauls at moderate charges.

80   *Advertisement for Barton's Garage, Clapham. Claude Barton was agent for the Ingleborough estate.*

Motor cars that chugged through the town had also to face the trauma of a climb on Buckhaw Brow, beyond which the road dipped steeply at Cave Ha'. When Fred Ellis went to the West Yorkshire Garage at Settle as an apprentice on 4 March 1912, paying a premium to learn the trade, local roads were still unmetalled. On a clear night, Fred, standing at the front of the garage, might see in the distance, gleaming white, a section of the road ascending Buckhaw Brow. In dry weather, a motorist looking back saw only a cloud of dust. The council began coating the main roads with tarmacadam in the early 1920s.

Fred's first job was to clean out a gearbox: 'The oil was like butter and you scraped it out with your hands.' The chief job turned out to be straightening axles, which was done at a forge, the air for which came from a device attached to a pedal. After the First World War the firm bought a 20-seater charabanc and ran trips to the Lancashire coastal resorts, the return fare for Morecambe being 5s. The vehicle, having solid tyres, shook a good deal. The driver hoped he would have plenty of notice of impending rain, for he had to stop the vehicle and erect a canvas hood.

In 1920, motorists using the Keighley-Kendal road began to patronise Barton's Garage at the village of Clapham. The proprietor, Claude Barton, was the agent of Ingleborough estate who, hearing Lloyd George begin to speak about the nationalisation of land, felt uncertain about his job and decided to have another in reserve. Estate men were employed in the construction of the hanger-like building. Barton's Garage was, for a time in the 1930s, the best-equipped between the industrial towns of the West Riding and Morecambe. A prime customer was Farrer, of Ingleborough Hall, who had a 1918 Austin saloon that, with Teddy Harrison at the wheel, regularly conveyed the family to their London home.

81   *Accident at Giggleswick, 1930s. A small saloon car has attempted to pass between a Leeds-bound bus and a northbound Settle Limes lorry.*

The garage's two petrol pumps were manipulated by hand. Cans of aviation spirit and benzole, needed for the sporty cars that drew up at Clapham, were kept just inside the main door, in case of fire. Essex cars were comparatively cheap imports from America, of the type that achieved notoriety through the activities of the gangster Al Capone and his men. Such cars were sold in moderate numbers at Clapham, each costing £260. Another of the proprietor's interests was caravanning. Coach-built and heavy, the caravans were hired or sold, Barton demonstrating their value in the 1920s when he towed a caravan to northern Scotland for a holiday. He hired out Eccles vans for between £6 and £9 a week, depending on size. The garage had an efficient service fitting tow-bars to motor cars.

Geoffrey Rowley, writing in 1969, considered that the advent of the motor car had probably affected Skipton more radically than the arrival of the canal or railway. The historic first appearance of a car locally took place on 9 April 1897, and a week later the *Craven Herald* reported, 'A motor car passed through the town on Friday morning and was again seen on its return on Saturday afternoon.' In the issue of the *Herald* for 11 August 1905, a writer considered that 'a motor car has more whims than a woman and, taken as a whole, they are more difficult to manage …'.

Skipton, the vehicle-packed 'gateway to the Dales', was eventually by-passed. So was Settle, where traffic problems remain acute, largely because there is no ready access to the by-pass for a vast number of quarry vehicles. Grassington is swamped by cars at busy times and, until recently, the peace of historic green lanes in Craven was shattered by the whine of motor vehicles.

Chapter 9

Industrial Growth

The High Corn Mill at Skipton was first used for that purpose in 1310. For centuries malt money was exacted from those who used the mill. (The Castle Estate was to own the mill until 1954, when it was acquired by a local man, George Leatt, who restored and repaired it.) The Earl of Thanet, keen to protect his own local interests, discouraged the acquisition of land on long-term lease for industrial development. A writer in the *Gentleman's Magazine* in 1794 described Skipton as a place 'thinly peopled, where trade has not yet spread affluence, nor the arts of civilisation polished the general manners or enlarged the sentiments of the inhabitants'. One of those who was keen to spread affluence was Titus Salt. In the 1840s, frustrated in his attempt to build his mills on a site at the bottom of the High Street, he switched his attention to a vacant site further down the Aire valley. Here, on a grand scale, he created Saltaire, comprising workplace and model village, with church but no pub.

82   *A North Craven tanyard. The market at Settle was once noted for its leather products.*

83 *Mill with shawled weavers, a popular view of the Industrial Revolution.*

The Thanet line came to an end with the death of the 11th Earl in 1849 and the Skipton estates passed to Sir Richard Tufton, who in 1851 was elevated to a baronetcy. He lived in Kent and visited Skipton infrequently. Little development had taken place except for a proliferation of public houses and the 'infilling' of the town's yards. The only new building sites were Union Square, Commercial Street and Spring Gardens. The appointment of Angus Nicholson as agent of the Castle Estate led to great changes. Nicholson, a canny Scot, persuaded Tufton to depart from the rigid policy of the past and to make land available freehold or on a generous 99-year lease. Some of the land so released was devoted to new housing schemes.

Industrial development proceeded apace between 1830 and 1880, following the completion of the canal and the arrival of the railway. The population increase, from 3,000 to 9,000 in 30 years following 1830, led to new development away from the town centre. Terraced housing was constructed on the south side of the town, near the canal and close to the mills. The censuses of 1831, 1841 and 1851 reveal that what had been a static population of 4,842 rose to 5,044 and fell again to 4, 962, but subsequently the rise in population was steady, a peak being reached in 1911 with a figure of 12,977. From 1860 until 1890, the area between the canal and the south side of the town was filled with a solid, if neat, mass of housing. The old Mill Field, part of the West Field, was developed following the making of the new Gargrave Road, which in the years following 1910 became a setting for middle-class housing.

The oldest textile enterprise was the High Mill in Castle Woods, built in 1785 for the 7th Earl of Thanet, who granted the lease to Peter Garforth, John Blackburn and John Sidgwick. Cotton yarns were produced. In 1786 work stopped for a time, following claims that the copying of details from Richard Arkwright's water-powered looms had breached patents. The claim being unsuccessful, Sidgwick was the sole lessee of the mill by 1806. Steam power was introduced in 1820 and in 1839 the Sidgwicks built Low Mill by the canal, off Sackville Street, where weaving and weft spinning took place. High Mill closed in 1890, when competition from the large mills that had sprung up in Lancashire proved too intense.

In the Craven Dales, the middle reaches of the rivers had many varied mills, all powered by waterwheel. Corn mills became cotton mills and, with the development of steam power, the rural cotton industry declined. At least 16 waterwheels existed between Beamsley and Grassington but little evidence remains for most of them. At Hartlington Mill, near Burnsall in Wharfedale, corn was ground; the premises were then enlarged for use as a cotton mill, which was run by the Ambler family. One of two mills at Hebden was used for weaving, power coming from a high breast type of waterwheel that had a diameter of about 26 feet. The mill stood idle for some years and the looms were scrapped. Then, with fresh looms and owners, weaving took place during and for a few years after the First World War.

Linton had its Little Worsted Mill, with a big wheel powered by water that had travelled three miles underground from Conistone Moor and then flowed into the Wharfe. Close by Linton Falls was a large weaving mill, water for the 12ft wide wheel being drawn from the river. Taken out in about 1920, the wheel was replaced by a turbine.

Handloom weaving was an important industry by 1800, when the clack and shutter of looms might be heard from the top floors of houses built with such weaving in mind. At Skipton, in 1808, three-storeyed cottages for handloom weavers appeared in the cobbled Union Square. Union Shed, dated 1867, the first mill to be built following the release of land by the Tuftons, had a canal-side site off Keighley Road. It was one of several enterprises to be rented to budding textile tycoons. A similar enterprise off Broughton Road was available in 1897 and, in the following year, Firth Mill was opened.

At Bradley, a village tucked away in a little side valley of the Aire, rather more than two miles south of Skipton, Charles Brown & Company, who had been operating in Cross Lane Mill, found themselves in dispute with the landlord and had to move so a new shed was proposed. The transfer from Cross Lane to Rose Shed was accomplished in 13 weeks, during which time there was a flurry of activity, with first-class stone for the new mill being quarried locally. The company taught the handloom weavers of Bradley the use of power looms but there was such feeling in the district against them that at first the Browns dare not let a weaver use more than two narrow looms.

The story of Skipton's textile industry was to be dominated by John Dewhurst. The firm was built up on cotton easily transported by canal from Liverpool and

84 *Red-brick chimney, Dewhurst's Mill, Skipton, and the Leeds and Liverpool Canal. The chimney was demolished and the mill is being converted to non-industrial uses.*

other west coast ports and drew in labour from rural areas, greatly augmenting the town's population. The Dewhurst climb to fame and fortune began when John had a cotton mill built at Airton in Malhamdale about 1838-40. It was a durable building, made of on-site limestone, with corner stones plucked from their ancient bed on the fell near Kirkby Malham. Then he moved to the banks of the canal abutting Union Square in Skipton, a resort of handloom weavers. Dewhurst introduced the first power looms into the town in 1829. Aware of the opposition from handloom weavers, whose livelihood was about to be affected, he had the looms transported to his mill in unmarked crates. Gutted by fire in 1831, the mill was rebuilt within six months.

Many writers on working conditions in cotton mills, especially in those employing children, have given horrific accounts. Frederic Montagu (1838) wrote a favourable account after visiting John Dewhurst's mill at Skipton, referring to Mr Dewhurst as 'a most humane and kind-hearted man'. Visiting the mill unannounced, he found 'the very perfection of order, regularity and cleanliness'. Air circulated freely and the children looked healthy, most of the girls being 'strong and well-figured'. It was a cheerful sort of environment.

Yet opposition to power looms grew in the minds of handloom operators as their livelihood diminished with industrialisation. Their grievances took a violent form at Skipton in 1842 when a large body of Lancashire men invaded the town in the so-called Plug-drawing Riots. The simple reasoning of the rioters was that they might stop the process that was putting them out of work by drawing the plugs from mill boilers. An estimated 3,000, marching four abreast and armed with sticks, tramped up the Broughton Road towards Dewhurst's mill. Most were content to bring the mills to a standstill but others toured the town, demanding money and looting shops and houses for food.

When a magistrate standing in the Market Place read the Riot Act, the rioters withdrew to Annahills, a field beside the Carleton road. The military, summoned from Burnley by a Skipton magistrate who had delivered the request on horseback, surrounded the mob and the Riot Act was read again. A quiet dispersal began, then someone flung a stone that fatally injured a soldier. Mr Garforth, one of the magistrates, was hit by another stone and lost an eye, and soldiers with fixed bayonets dispersed the mob. The soldiers were then summoned to Colne, where another disturbance was reported. Into Skipton, to keep order until calm was restored, came a company of the 73rd Regiment to be quartered in the Castle. The mills were kept running.

By 1854 John Dewhurst owned a weaving shed with 385 looms. When control of the business passed to his son, John Bonny Dewhurst, the major problem was the American Civil War, which had interfered with the supply of cotton. A slump was experienced in numerous mills throughout east Lancashire and West Yorkshire, but the Dewhursts flourished because they had a distinctive product. By treating cotton thread with sodium hydroxide, they gave it a lustrous appearance not unlike spun silk. Sylko, the name given to this wondrous material, was a combination of the words silk and cotton.

85 *Model of a Lancashire power loom, the type commonly used in northern weaving sheds.*

86 *A typical weaving shed, with rows of Lancashire looms.*

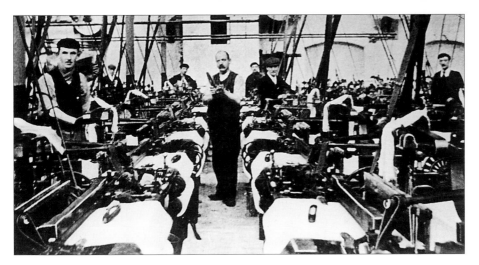

With sharply rising trade, the Belle Vue Mill, a five-storey structure with outlying buildings and some 20,000 square yards of floorspace, rose beside the Broughton Road, becoming the workplace of over 800 people. The mill ran for the first time on 4 February 1870. A contributor to the *Craven Herald* in October 1874, enthusing about the new factory, mentioned rooms that were large, lofty, well-lighted and adequately ventilated. John Bonny Dewhurst and his family lived a grand life at their mansion in Aireville Park, within sight of the mill and its lofty red-brick chimney. In 1897 the firm became one of 14 concerns forming the English Sewing Cotton Company.

Union Shed, off Keighley Road, built in 1867, was one of two mills constructed with the view to leasing its room and power to small tenants. Firth Mill, in Sackville Street, was opened in 1878 by Samuel Farey, who had arrived in town in 1844 to become head of the British School, from which job he switched to weaving, and

87   *Carnival day at Langcliffe High Mill, Settle, today devoted to paper products.*

88   *Langcliffe millworkers, c.1910. They were summoned to work by mill steam whistle – and fined, if late.*

then mill-owning. W.H. Dawson tells us that 'here are manufactured windeys and dyed cotton goods for the Bradford and Manchester markets'. George Walton built a large shed on the canal bank in Keighley Road for himself in 1877-8, and Dawson reported that 'the premises comprise weaving shed (holding 500 looms), warehouses, weft-room, engine and boiler houses, finishing room and offices, standing upon 3,300 square yards of ground'. Here were manufactured 'dress goods, skirtings and shirtings'.

Mark Nutter, who took over Mr Farey's mill in 1925, produced rayon umbrella material, and during the Second World War switched effortlessly to making parachute material. After more than a century of activity, during which time textiles were the major employer at Skipton, the industry succumbed, between the 1960s and the 1980s, to cheaper foreign imports. Most of the mills have since been adapted as blocks of flats.

89   *A small country textile mill, Bradley, near Skipton. The Green family owned it.*

A Settle resident, Ellwood Brockbank, used three textile mills – none of them in Craven! – for his innovation of shopping by post, which is now an accepted part of modern life. Using the slogan 'Fireside Shopping', which he registered, he bought goods at wholesale prices from the firms for postal distribution among retail customers. A trade paper of the 1880s 'heartily recommended' the Brockbank system of shopping without leaving home. Ellwood was born into a Quaker family at Salford and educated at Ackworth but left in 1854 on the unexpected death of his father. In the following year he was working as an assistant to John Tatham & Sons, who were grocers with premises in Settle. Eventually Ellwood was running the firm, but he had enough energy to open separate premises where he pioneered his shopping by post, concentrating on links with firms in Lancashire (for dress fabrics), in Somerset (for serges) and in Northern Ireland (for linens). Boxes of patterns were sent free to inquirers. Goods were ordered strictly for cash, with no discount, and supplied direct by return carriage (or postage paid) to all parts of Britain.

Chapter 10

Mineral, Flags and Limestone

The Craven Dales were almost turned inside out in the quest for materials that could be marketed. Limestone blasted from Hawbank, also known as Skipton Rock, was quarried on a grand scale. In late Victorian times nearly a hundred quarrymen were employed and, until the opening of the Springs Canal, the stone was carted through the town to the basin of the Leeds and Liverpool Canal. Grassington Moor had its natural state gravely disturbed in the quest for lead. Tales were told of the Knockers, mysterious beings dwelling in the mines who helpfully gave warning of any accident that was about to occur.

When the author first ventured on to Greenhow Hill, between Wharfedale and Nidderdale, in the mid-1950s, he found abundant evidence of the old mining days. There were derelict mine buildings, the crumbling entrances to long-vacated mine levels and even a rusty clog iron half buried in peat to remind him of the human aspect. Greenhow, on a tongue of limestone, the edge of which was distorted by geological faulting, was highly mineralised. Past generations of leadminers were collectively known as 't'Old Man'.

Sixty years ago, when the demand for local lead had gone, Fred Walker, a descendant of the Greenhow leadminers, and others, sifted through heaps of spoil seeking fluorspar for the steel industry, a vibrating board having been devised to remove the last traces of lead. Elsewhere in Craven, a large deposit of calamine (zinc carbonate) was

90 *Smelt mill chimney, Malham Moor. Like several others in Craven, the ancient masonry has been stabilised.*

mined in Pikedaw, between Settle and Malham. A chance discovery by miners looking for lead was a cave passage packed with calamine, which was in demand by makers of brass.

An incongruous feature in a landscape of heather, grouse and millstone outcrops on Fountains Fell is a stone coke oven relating to a long-expired colliery. The coal – thin, brittle stuff in the Yoredale Series of rocks – was extracted using bell-pits. At Helwith Bridge, a blue flagstone of Silurian origin was quarried and sawn into pieces and used widely in water cisterns, shelves and flooring in houses and on farms, as well as for vats at breweries in Yorkshire and Northern Ireland. Elsewhere in Ribblesdale, quarrying exposed high quality limestone.

91   *Reconstruction of a typical lead-mining lodging-place.*

The quest for lead involved hundreds of people spread over thousand of acres, the main orefields being on Grassington Moor and Greenhow Hill. Thomas Dunham Whitaker, in *History of Craven* (1805), did not know of a greater calamity that might befall a village than the discovery of a lead mine in the neighbourhood. Arthur Young (1770) considered that leadminers were fickle: they 'could scarcely, by any means, be kept to the performance of a regular business'. The lead sought in Craven originated with liquids emanating from deep in the earth which were squeezed into cracks in limestone and gritstone. Most of the galena-rich veins, distributed haphazardly and almost vertically, ranged in thickness from a few inches to the extensive deposit, at a depth of over 100ft, known as an 'ore shoot'. In the Grassington-Greenhow mining field, the Bycliffe vein, as described by Raistrick, extended from the edge of Conistone Moor to near Pateley Bridge, a length of at least nine miles.

Surface features include flues leading to moortop chimneys. Leats (water channels) and dams testify to the copious amounts of water needed to turn powerful waterwheels. Raistrick believed that the development of mining into the position of a major industry was made possible largely by their use. Their first application was on the smelting side. 'As early as the 15th century, a waterwheel was commonly used to move the bellows for a small furnace.' The workings on Grassington Moor had a complex management system. In the 1820s Blea Beck was dammed three times and flowed across the moor in a clay-lined leat to yet another dam, which provided power for two waterwheels concerned with pumping and winding. The watercourse continued for two more miles, powering a crushing mill at Yarnbury, and then other systems were fed before it poured into Hebden Gill.

Unorganised mining is probably older than Roman times, but evidence for it has not been recognised. Raistrick recorded the discovery, sometime before 1885, of a pig of lead with a Trajan inscription on Nussey Knott, between Greenhow Hill and Hebden, and theorised that it must belong to the period about 98 A.D. Documentary evidence from monastic times, when much lead was needed to roof the new monasteries, is mainly concerned with the orefield of the northern dales, especially Swaledale.

The Craven connection seems to have begun with a grant by Roger de Mowbray to Fountains Abbey of lead mines in the manors of Bewerley and Dacre – on Greenhow Hill, in fact. Here the extremity of the Craven district was to be marked by a stone cross. In 1300 Bolton Priory purchased the manor of Appletreewick, opening mines in Mungo Gill, also on Greenhow. About 1603 the Earl of Cumberland, one of the Cliffords, transferred miners from his undertakings in Derbyshire to open and extend mines on Yarnbury and Grassington Moor. A smelt mill was constructed by the Wharfe, almost opposite Linton church. The Procter family, who acquired much of the land held by Fountains at the Dissolution, extended the mines at Greenhow and Appletreewick Moor.

William Camden, a 16th-century antiquarian who toured the dale country, wrote, 'the hills afford great store of lead'. He was thinking in particular of Swaledale, but lead was mined extensively in the aforementioned areas, and in the vicinity of Kettlewell, Malham and Cononley. On Malham Moor, the Richgroves mine was driven from a gill below Pikedaw. This level, which was being worked in 1751, survived intermittently into the 19th century. The mine was a major talking point in 1887 when a block of ore weighing a ton was removed from it. The Lister family of Gisburne Park eventually owned all the mines.

It is assumed that mining in the Kilnsey and Littondale area started on Hawkswick Moor about 1697, the ore being transported to a smelt mill at Grassington. About 1730 a smelt mill of modest size was constructed at Kilnsey to deal with ores from small workings on Kilnsey Moor and High Mark. The mines situated on the lower slopes of Great Whernside and on Buckden Pike were worked over a long period but were never major producers of lead ore, the main workings being set in and around Dowber Gill. Shortly after 1699 a smelt mill constructed by the Trust Lords of Kettlewell, at the foot of the Gill, was in use, also smelting ores from the Conistone and Starbotton mines. In the 17th century, leadminers who had previously slogged from their homes in Pateley Bridge and other low-lying places were permitted to have intake holdings on Greenhow Hill, many such holdings providing horses or ponies for underground mine haulage and for pack transport on the surface.

Also at this time, deposits of lead in Upper Wharfedale were being tapped via bell pits, deep shafts and long levels being excavated at Kettlewell. A bell pit was a shaft of around 25 or 30 feet that was opened out when the lead vein was struck. By the closing years of the 17th century, a honeycomb effect had been created by levels and shafts extending to a depth at which work was stopped by water. When the Craven Cross mines on Greenhow were flooded, the owners sought advice from Smeaton,

92   *Harald Bruff, who recorded the lives of leadminers on Greenhow.*

designer of the Eddystone Lighthouse, and in 1784 they bought a Boulton and Watt steam engine, feeding it with local coal.

Pumping water from the mines on Grassington Moor being costly, Mr Flint, an imaginative agent of the Duke of Devonshire in the late 1780s, proposed a radical solution, a 'boat level' driven from Hebden Gill. It would run at a greater depth than had yet been reached by shafts, solving the current water problem and penetrating new ground. Begun in 1796, when Mr Bowden was agent, what became known as the Duke's Level had grand dimensions, being nine feet high and five feet wide. In the 1800s, when John Taylor was the Duke's chief mineral agent, he ended the concept of a boat level, reducing its dimensions to that of an adit level. Additions were made to the grand plan and work continued for 28 years at a cost to the Duke of £33,000.

The early smelting process involved furnaces with wood as fuel. In the late 16th century ore-hearth smelting became the norm. This small-scale blast furnace used bellows driven by waterwheel, the fuel being a combination of peat and dry wood. A good smelter might produce about a ton of lead in a shift of between 10 and 12 hours. As time went by, the number of hearths was increased. A special hearth, using coke as fuel, was used to recover lead from slag. Poisonous fumes were led away from the smelters along flues that ran uphill to chimneys. Flags lining the flues cooled the hearth gases. Lead condensing out in the soot was recovered by being scraped out and amounted to about five per cent of the total yield. Two condenser houses were included in a flue on Grassington Moor, the scrapings being flushed by water into settling ponds.

Workers in the Craven lead mines appear to have been mainly of Yorkshire stock, as one might suppose, augmented by immigrants from Scotland, Ireland and Cornwall. Dickinson notes that at Greenhow Hill in the 19th century there was a large floating contingent of Welsh males. 'In build they tended to be tall and large-boned, not particularly suited to the cramped conditions of the mine workings.' Mostly, they lived within walking distance of home, although with the expansion of the industry rows of cottages specifically for mining families were built at Grassington and Hebden. Accommodation problems at Cononley were eased when, in 1832, a local building society was formed and a row of cottages was constructed for those associated with the mines.

93 *Commemorative portrait of Harald Bruff, of Greenhow Hill.*

The men's wages were erratic, whether they worked for a direct wage or followed the 'laws and customs' introduced in Derbyshire and applied on the Earl's ground on Grassington Moor. Under this system, several men formed a partnership and bargained with the agent for work to be done and ore to be produced. The system endured for most of the 19th century. Harald John Lexhow Bruff, who lived among the 'oade 'uns' of Greenhow and made a name for himself writing character sketches, noted that part of a vein was let off to a man or gang of men. These were partners, being paid at so much a 'bing' (about 8 cwt), which was then the standard measure for cleaned or dressed lead ore. The lowest bidder would be the 'take' for a month.

In townships where mining was undertaken in an organised way, the first person to discover a vein had a right to work it for two 'meres', adjacent 'meres' being worked by others. A 'mere' was, by common consent, the distance a hammer might be thrown. On Grassington Moor, where customary mining law is best known, Raistrick recorded inscriptions on mere stones. Two examples are 'Geo. Fletcher & Co.' and 'John Barker & Co. Founder'.

When miners following lead veins had to go underground, the great problem was the disposal of waste. This was achieved by 'stoping': if a vein were overhead, waste could be trampled on; if it were underfoot, then ways had to be found of stacking it. One solution was to make a timber framework or stone arching above which the waste could be placed.

The old-time miner expected to get wet. If he spent time looking for a dry spot in a mine he would not get much work done. When at rest, having his 'snap' (food), he invariably sat on the heels of his clogs to keep out the water. He worked by candlelight, which he attached to a wall with a lump of clay. In 'black spots', short of air, a candle would not burn. He was fond of 'bacca' (tobacco), having heard that folks never felt hungry as long as they had plenty to 'chaw' (chew) and 'reek' (smoke). Bruff spoke of a miner called Fast who sang in the mine (if anyone whistled while underground, luck would be driven away) and loved his work so much that in his spare time he would roam about the abandoned workings that cut through the upper part of the hill, seeking clues that might lead him to lost veins.

Many miners died while still in their forties of Gruver's disease, a respiratory complaint caused by a confined, dusty environment. Asthmatics who had inhaled too much powder-smoke spat black. Those who lived beyond the age of 40 found lighter work. Of the three public houses on Greenhow, the aptly named *Miners Arms* was the most important, serving as a social centre for the scattered village and a venue for discussing the mines and, more specifically, the bargains between men and owners. Miners born locally were serious-minded men who enjoyed reading, went to chapel on Sunday and from 1820 sent their children to a school that had been built by subscription.

Bailey J. Harker, visiting a lead mine, recounted his experiences in his book *Upper Wharfedale* (1869). Ladders and ropes were being used. Safely down, he was led by one of the miners into different 'levels' and handed a candle set in a piece of clay 'to keep your hand from melting the tallow by its warmth'. He was called upon to ramble among rocks, to wade through water and march through mud. He crept through holes, squeezed through a tortuous crevice, then moved on all fours, 'bear fashion', crawling, scrambling and struggling to where the rich veins of lead might be seen, 'glinting and sparkling like jewels in the rock'. He was also shown 'little caverns of spar' and thus was more than rewarded for his toil.

The miner got the 'bouse' (a mixture of rock, spar and ore) out by what Raistrick described as 'a mixture of picks, hammers, drills and a variety of wedges'. In the early 18th century gunpowder was being used, and the practice had become common by mid-century. The 'bouse' was moved to the shaft by 'shovels, sledges, wheelbarrows or wheeled trucks on light rails'. The process of preparing it for smelting was

94 *Stump Cross Caverns, Greenhow, discovered by miners and opened up to the public.*

known as 'dressing', and involved sorting into walled bays known as 'bousesteads' or 'bouse teams'. The 'bouse', having been crushed into small uniform pieces, initially to the size of peas with 'buckers' (heavy, short-shafted hammers), and later with cast-iron rollers, was dressed in an appliance called a 'buddle'. Agitated in water on a fine sieve, the mixed ore and spar separated, the ore sinking to the bottom, the spar coming to the top and being scraped off.

95 *George Gill, for many years owner-guide at Stump Cross Caverns.*

The Duke of Devonshire opened up a lead mine on the moors above Cononley and Glusburn. The main vein outcropped on Gib, where the chimney and what remained of a smelt mill have been conserved. Work at the mine augmented for some local folk an income that had previously relied entirely on farming and cottage textiles. As labour was imported from Cornwall, Derbyshire and Wales, the total population rose to 1,500 people. The production of lead had virtually ended by 1869, following which time small quantities were lifted to meet specific orders.

Lead mining in Craven declined in the 1880s. In the following decade the price of lead was at the low point of £9 10s. a ton and cheaper lead was being imported. Some miners took their families to the industrialised towns of the North East or

96 *The Old Colliery at Ingleton. Coal was mined at various places in the district.*

east Lancashire, finding work in textile mills or coal mines. A number emigrated to the remoter parts of what was then the British Empire. Between thirty and forty Greenhow men were working at the Craven Cross mine when the decision was taken to close it down. Mining continued for a spell in the 1920s but the following years were spent abstracting fluorspar from the old spoil heaps.

It was a joy to listen to old-timers recount tales of 't'oade 'uns upuv Greenho'. Fred Walker, a descendant of Greenhow miners who lived at Dry Ghyll, a building that was once *The Grouse Inn*, had heard that on a patch of grass beside the road a leadminer called Joss fought Gipsy Jack – and won. During the fight, which was over a horse deal, much blood was shed. Fred Longthorn, who at 85 lived alone in a house standing at an elevation of 1,300 feet, told me of a miner living at Pateley Bridge who ascended 1,000 feet in the four-mile walk to Greenhow. He made a point of arriving at his workplace at about 5.30 a.m. and rested a while before starting work with the 6 a.m. shift. Early last century, there were eight or nine miles of underground wagon roads at the mines, according to Fred, who added: 'You travel right over the top of some of them when you use the main road. Some of the workings were 120 yards deep.'

George Gill, a former owner of Stump Cross Cave, discovered in 1860, explained that a party of Greenhow miners sinking trial shafts and hoping to locate a rich vein of lead found a natural opening at a depth of over forty feet but, as it was time for a meal, settled down to eat. Two small boys who were working with them crawled underground, alternately walking and splashing through water. They reached a large chamber that held calcite formations of great size and, rushing back to the miners, said, 'We've seen a lot of naked men leaning against a wall.' Stump Cross is now a major tourist attraction.

97   *Blue Flag Quarry at Helwith Bridge.*

Copper ore was mined at Pikedaw Hill, above Malham. Thomas Hurtley, the Malham schoolmaster, in his concise history of the locality, published the earliest notice in 1786. Describing Gennett's Cave (at what is now called Janet's Foss), he refers to 'the Smelters of a valuable Mine of Copper from Pikedaw in the Manor of West-Malham, then belonging to the Lambert Family jointly with the ancestors of its present Possessors. To this day there are the evident Ruins of a Smelt Mill.' Hurtley had no doubt that there existed 'in these Manors' many rich and invaluable veins both of lead and other minerals. Raistrick, commenting that the smelting of copper is one of the most difficult technical processes, observed that locally it was 'roasted', not smelted.

The Lamberts sold their Malham estates to Thomas Lister (1752-1826), subsequently the 1st Lord Ribblesdale, who had a grand house at Gisburn. His agent, both for the estates and mines, was the Rev. Thomas Collins. Happily for future historians, Collins was an inveterate letter writer. Unhappily for mining, he had no personal knowledge of the industry. When the Ribblesdale line died out, Tot Lord, a Settle antiquary, bought many letters and made them available to Arthur Raistrick. Nonetheless, little is known about the copper mines, which were being worked in the late 1780s.

Miners broke through into a natural cavity of such size it was dubbed the Great Gulph or the Great Shake. Many of the copper deposits were found in irregular veins. The importance of the Great Gulph was the amount of calamine (zinc carbonate) lying just beyond it. A successful application to mine the stuff was made to William Brayshaw of Malham, who held the lease on the Malham Moor mines. Collins, the agent, employed relatively few miners, recruiting them from the coal mines around Burnley (where he was rector). Until 1798, vast quantities of calamine were transported to Cheadle Brass Company of Stafford using the new canal system. About 1830, when the deposits in the main caverns were almost exhausted, miners were diverted to the Fountains Fell colliery and others found work mining lead.

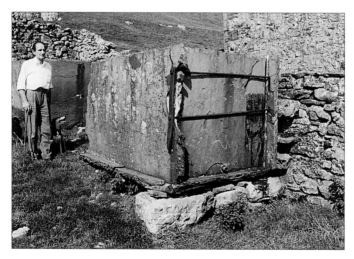

98   Water cistern made of Blue Flag, Malhamdale.

99　*Limestone quarry on Giggleswick Scar, which the Spencer family owned.*

Before the railways were transporting coal to the Craven area from the deep mines of South Yorkshire, it was sought locally. Most of the seams were thin and the coal was brittle. Men who had been mining calamine operated the colliery on Fountains Fell from 1807. Raistrick recorded that a borehole driven near the tarn on Fountains Fell penetrated 170 feet of grit and shale, in which were five beds of coal. Three seams had a thickness of four inches, one seam was three inches thick, and at a depth of 160 feet was a seam of 2ft 4½in; these were worked using shafts. In the shale at the highest part of Fountains Fell was a bed of weathered coal about 2ft 6in thick that was suited to being used in the many field kilns where limestone was burned to sweeten local fields. The seam was within reach of bell pits sunk to between twenty or thirty feet, the coal being wound up by a hand-operated jack-roller winch. In 1810 deeper shafts were being sunk to reach the better quality coal. Coal of the best quality was fed to the unique, stone-built coke oven.

Coal was mined in a small way at several places in the Ingleton district. They included Wilson Wood Pit (closed in 1887), Dolands Main, Grove Pit and, earlier, Maggie Pit, Jin Pit and Moorgarth Pit. In 1913, a survey at the edge of the village led to the excavation of two shafts. It was the start of the New Colliery, which would take advantage of the nearness of a railway station. The colliery was to operate fitfully for only 25 years. The engineers located seams of a depth of 9 feet and 10 feet that had previously escaped notice, but they had not reckoned with the trickery of the Craven Fault, which cut off the seams to the east, and the Hollin Tree Fault, running from the mines to Burton-in-Lonsdale.

The colliery was saved by the First World War when the government took over the country's mines and guaranteed the Ingleton owners a 7½ per cent profit. The

100   *Langcliffe Quarry, showing the chimney of the Hoffman-type kiln, where lime-burning was continuous.*

number of workers rose sharply until about 500 men were employed between 1917 and 1920. In one week over 2,000 tons of coal were lifted. A ton of coal cost 18s. and local people might fill a handcart for 2s. The colliery was closed during the General Strike. Quakers organised subscriptions from abroad, chiefly from America, in order to level a large pit heap near the main road and screen the land with trees, and Ingleton Colliery closed permanently in 1937.

A colliery on Threshfield Moor turned out to be one of the less rewarding enterprises of John Delaney. When it was closed, in November 1905, it had lasted for less than a decade, the pumps installed being incapable of dealing with the inflow of water, and Delaney suffered a loss of about £30,000. The colliery was situated at an elevation of 890 feet, the depth of the shaft being 65 feet. A gravity, rope-hauled tramway ran for 4,160 feet down the hillside to Delaney's quarries, which lay some 200 feet below.

These quarries owed their existence to the proximity of the Skipton to Grassington branch line, completed in July 1902. Wagons used at the quarry were similar to those in the colliery, a splendid example of integration. The coming of the Settle-Carlisle Railway in 1876 – and, earlier, the line between Skipton and Morecambe via Giggleswick – enabled best quality, deep-mined coal from South Yorkshire to be available in North Craven and John Delaney became the main distributor of coal. With his lime quarries, he owned over a thousand private railway wagons. Some, bearing his name, were still to be seen in North Ribblesdale until the Second World War.

Horton Flags, underlying Moughton Fell in North Ribblesdale, was worked in five little quarries at Helwith Bridge. A rock of the Silurian age, hard, fine-grained and blueish, it splits into slabs of great size but no great thickness. An early reference to flag production appears in a statement outlining the case for a canal for Settle in

1774. The writer mentions 'many inexhaustible quarries of blue-flags, grit flags, excellent blue slate and grit-slate in the neighbourhood of Settle, which will undoubtedly pass along this canal'. The canal was never constructed. Coombs Quarry, above Foredale, is historically important, being visited by John Hutton, the clergyman-author of *Tour to the Caves* (1780). Hutton noticed that 'the stones are of a blue kind, like slate, from one to three inches thick; some are two or three yards broad, and five or six yards long.'

In early times such slabs proved ideal for clapper-bridges across local becks. Broader pieces were laid on beds of sand to provide durable floors in farmhouses. Blue Flag, impervious to liquid and therefore easily cleaned, was used widely as 'binks' (shelves) in dairies. Trimmed slabs were conveyed from Helwith Bridge to breweries at Tadcaster, where they were re-assembled as vats. The stone was widely used in the Craven Dales for 'boskins' (divisions between stalls) in shippons, for gate stoops, lintels on houses and even tombstones in local churchyards. In limestone country, where water is hard, cisterns made of pieces of flag jointed and bound by iron held the 'soft' rainwater draining from roofs for use domestically, but not for drinking, it being customary to seal the joints using white or red lead. The trough-ends were held taut by bars and bolts fitted by the local blacksmith.

At Helwith Bridge, at a riverside sawmill which derived its power from a water-wheel, flagstones transported from the quarry face by low trucks on rails were sawn to the requisite sizes using a piece of iron with a straight edge which was worked backwards and forwards, with sand and water as an abrasive. By the 1920s the demand for flagstone came from farmers acquiring loads of cheap 'throughs' for their walls, or from a sentimental person seeking a piece of flag as a tombstone.

By the end of the 18th century, many limestone areas in Craven were smudged by the smoke from kilns where limestone was burnt, then spread in order to neutralise acid soils. A copious spread of lime, followed by hard grazing, was a means of bringing moorland intake into pasture. Lime was also needed domestically and for making mortar. The field kiln, a common feature in limestone areas, was used mainly

101　*Traction engine conveying limestone from the quarry to Giggles-wick railway station.*

between 1750 and 1850. Coal was needed but the coal transported from Fountains Fell, being impure, gave off bad gas.

Raistrick related how an old farmer in Wharfedale collecting lime at a kiln on Greenhow Hill would set out soon after midnight with horse and cart, to walk eight miles over rough ways, but his early start meant that on his return to the farm he still had enough time to fit in a full day's work. As a boy in the Aire valley, Raistrick visited a kiln on the canalside to buy a twopenny lump of fresh lime (a bucketful) in order to make whitewash for the annual spring cleaning.

Many limekilns were operating in the townships of Giggleswick and Settle in the 18th century, and farmers in the western part of the parish bought their lime from independent lime-burners mainly to be found on Giggleswick Scar. A small kiln was built at the foot of Castleberg, the limestone crag that dominates Settle, and John Hutton, in his *Tour of the Caves*, heard that the inhabitants, afraid that if any more were dug out the rock might fall and 'bury the whole town in ruins', had the lime-burner presented at the court of the manor. Twelve wise men, empanelled as jurors, concluded that if the rock fell it would tumble away from the town! In the later 18th century it was customary in the many Turnpike Acts and Enclosure Awards to make provision for the carriage of lime.

Michael Wilson (1816-91), a notable but almost forgotten quarryman, was concerned with lime workings at Ingleton and in North Ribblesdale. With the opening of the Little North Western Railway, Wilson and John Clark organised excursion trains for local people and with the proceeds acquired a contract for the use of the old limekiln in Austwick. Realising that the biggest demand for lime would be from customers outside the district, they arranged with the railway company for a siding to be built at Laneside, on the Settle side of Clapham station, from which lime could be transported. The partners dealt in timber and then leased the kilns beside Giggleswick Scar, fuelling them with Fountains Fell coal that was transported to Giggleswick by pack pony.

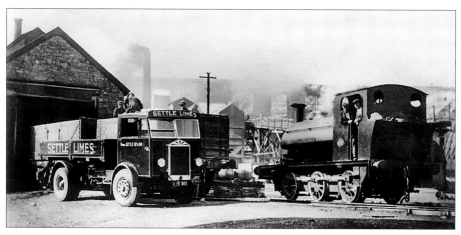

102   *Horton Limeworks.*

103   *Horton
Limeworks, developed
by John Delaney,
much of the lime being
despatched by rail.*

When the lease ran out, they transferred their attention to Mealbank, Ingleton. The right to Mr Hoffman's patent 'for lime burning within a limited area' was acquired in the 1850s. The Hoffman kiln they constructed had 18 chambers to which there were 30 feeding holes for coal and coke. It was able to burn limestone continuously, the fire moving from chamber to chamber and the flue extending to a tall chimney at the crest of the nearest hill. The maximum production was 60 tons of lime a day. A new company had been formed, consisting of Messrs Clark, Wilson, Charlesworth and Shepherd. Wilson's daughter, Amelia, aged ten, had the responsibility for taking £100 by train from Giggleswick to Ingleton to pay the wages of employees at the lime works.

Wilson became a director of the Stainforth Lime Works, in North Ribblesdale, whose company chairman, Lorenzo Christie, owned mills between Settle and Lang-cliffe. A Hoffman-type kiln being in use at Ingleton already, it was decided to build another, three times the size, at Langcliffe, which would be a modification of the original, for improved efficiency. Its completion in 1873 was celebrated by Michael Wilson, with Amelia sitting on his knee, being raised in a 'bucket' to the top of the chimney. Wilson died in his sleep on 2 April 1891 and was buried at Clapham in a plot where, five years before, his wife Agnes had been laid to rest.

John Delaney, who opened up two of the largest limestone quarries in Craven, was born in Ireland in 1846. John's father, an estate agent with the thankless job of collecting rents from starving tenants following the failure of the potato crop, was shot by a band of rebellious smallholders. Ann, the eldest daughter, settled the family at Stalybridge in Cheshire. John eventually took a job at Christie's Mill in North Ribblesdale and quickly rose to become an overseer. In 1870 he married Annie Calver, a Lancashire weaver. In his spare time he began trading in a variety of goods. Following the opening of the Settle-Carlisle Railway he dealt in coal, his capital of £40 being provided by an old Quaker banker in Settle. The banker was also a guide and a friend and in 1876 John applied to join the Society of Friends. His Quaker convictions were apparent in every aspect of his life.

104   *Workers at a Ribblesdale limestone quarry.*

At the mill he was told by the manager to work for them or for himself and he chose the latter, buying a small general store in Langcliffe and leaving his wife to run it, then heading for Manchester University to read geology and discover how he might exploit the vast deposits of pure limestone in North Ribblesdale. He did this through quarrying and by using the railway to bring in coal and take away his limestone, which was in high demand at the steel works of Sheffield.

John moved his wife and daughter from Langcliffe to Settle in the 1890s. He developed Beecroft Quarry at Horton and an equally vast quarry near Threshfield, in Upper Wharfedale. He paid good wages and refused to lay off labour in slack times, finding them sundry jobs and paying full wages at the week's end. During the First World War he was in trouble with the authorities for his outspoken denunciation of the war. The magazine *John Bull* ran a scathing article denouncing his employment of German internees in the quarries. One of them, named Max, became a key man. John Delaney died on Christmas Day 1921 and, in his will, he left £5 to every workman in his employment.

Beecroft Quarry continues to provide high quality limestone. Stone is also quarried at Giggleswick Scar where, years ago, lime was transported in buckets on an overhead system that culminated at railway sidings. A large, ultra-modern quarry at Swindon, in Upper Wharfedale, makes use of the remaining section of the old Grassington Railway.

Chapter 11

A Victorian Town

Victoria acceded to the throne on 20 June 1837. On the following day the first foundation stone of Christ Church, Skipton was laid and a new Skipton parish was created. The populace sang 'God Save the King' even though he was already dead, the news having not yet filtered through to a town that had scarcely outgrown its old status of village. Improvements were in hand and a toll road to Draughton had been created, speeding on their way anyone who was heading for York. This avoided Shode Bank and the moor-edge route that had been used since Roman times, if not before. The old road had scared visitors to Skipton who felt as if they almost fell into the town.

The New Line (now prosaically known as Gargrave Road) ran beside parkland where stood a mansion known as Aireville, built for Henry Alcock in 1836 on a scale worthy of a local celebrity. Alcock's life was to span most of the Victorian age and his active interest would be felt in virtually every organisation of note. He was a solicitor and a partner in the Craven Bank, owned many properties in the town and drew an appreciable amount in rent, presided over the gas and water companies and also the North Western Railway Company, and served as a trustee of the Skipton Building Society.

105   *Skipton High Street in horse and cart days.*

When a survey revealed that 424 local families, totalling 1,781 people, had an income averaging 1s. 10½d. a week, Henry Alcock flaunted his wealth by acquiring a sedan chair to convey his two daughters to school at Lascelles Hall. The footmen who carried the chair wore plush knee breeches, canary-coloured waistcoats and cut-away swallow-tailed coats. When the young ladies were being transported to evening parties the footmen powdered their hair. Alcock had prestige and money but declining health led him to overwinter on the continent and he was abroad when he died just before Christmas in 1869. An obituary in the *Pioneer* gave him a foremost place among the gentry of the neighbourhood. His widow commemorated him in 1874 by donating £1,000 to buy a reredos for Holy Trinity Church.

In 1837 Skipton was not much more than a large village, with a population of about four thousand. Packhorses were still making their rounds and there were as yet no rail links with Leeds or Bradford or with east Lancashire. The pace of life seemed to quicken once or twice a week with the passage of a stagecoach. George Kendall, an old man, reflecting on what Skipton was like at the time, concluded the place was 'rather closed against advancement'. No land might be purchased and the small industries could not be extended, so many families had to leave town, seeking employment abroad.

The last of the earls of Thanet, who died in 1849, had been an absentee landlord. The trustees to whom the estate passed administered them for Richard Tufton, who attained the rank of baron, and subsequently for his natural son, Henry James, who was

106   *Skipton High Street on Show Day, 1870.*

ennobled as Lord Hothfield. Skipton had an absentee vicar, the Rev. John Parry, the last man to hold the office, having gone mad in 1778 and his successor, the Rev. John Perin, preferring to live at Kildwick. Holy Trinity Church was left in the care of a curate. The Rev. William Sidgwick, headmaster of Ermysted's Grammar School, was inactive through ill health but this gave him plenty of time to reflect on the status given to his family when Minnie, a sister, married the Archbishop of Canterbury. His brother, John Benson Sidgwick, had appointed a new governess in 1839. She came from Haworth and her name was Charlotte Brontë.

Another strong link between Skipton and the Brontës was my own great-great-grandfather, Dr William Cartman. He was born in Ripon in 1800, moved to Bingley as usher of the Grammar School and was ordained by the Archbishop of York to the curacy of Bingley, and thence

107   Dr William Cartman, Victorian head-master of Ermysted's Grammar School.

to Skipton, as assistant to Sidgwick, headmaster of Ermysted's. He succeeded him in this position in 1841 and held it until 1867. Among his friends and fellow clerics in the Bingley area had been Patrick Brontë, who, holding the living of Haworth, invited him to preach in Haworth church. The friendship blossomed to the extent that Cartman gave the oration at the funeral of Charlotte and was to join the Vicar of Bradford in conducting the funeral service of Patrick.

At Skipton, Cartman presided over a school of modest size situated by the beck at the bottom of Shode Bank. Gibbon, in his history of the school, noted that the headmaster kept numbers quite high (varying from about 40 to 90) but probably only succeeded in this by generous concessions to the anti-Latin element, his compromise solution being that each boy should receive instruction in Latin 'according to his ability'. This split the school into two departments, the smallest consisting of those being taught Latin. His teaching seems to have been popularised in verse. When the boys asked him on what day in December 1864 he proposed to begin the Christmas break, he replied:

> One sixth, one fourth, when joined to four,
> Will give the day, less half a score.
> The day o'th' month, no doubt;
> So now prepare your Lessons well,
> And you shall write your friends to tell...

108   *Skipton on Hospital Gala Day.*

At one time the staff of the school was drawn entirely from the Cartman family. Dr Cartman married well, his bride, Hannah O'Callaghan Pleasance, being connected with the banking family of Alcock of Aireville Hall. But, in June 1867, Cartman resigned his headship of Ermysted's Grammar School and no reason for his resignation was given. In September of that year he was at Portobello, near Edinburgh, in charge of St Mark's Episcopal Church, and there was the whiff of scandal. His companion in Scotland was a French lady who had been employed as a maid at Ermysted's.

At a time when critical attention was being given to the problem of secondary education, and many grammar schools closed their doors, Ermysted's survived, largely because of its large endowment. Gibbon examined the fate of four neighbouring grammar schools – Earby, Burnsall, Kirkby Malham and Bolton Abbey – which all became elementary schools and would eventually send boys to Skipton's grammar school.

The 19th century was a time of self-improvement for the working man, especially in the industrialised north. In the dying years of the 18th century, Dr George Birkbeck, a native of Settle, organised a series of free lectures for working-class folk at Anderson's Institution in Glasgow, the start of a movement leading to Mechanics' Institutes, a prime educational force. In the mid-19th century over 300 Institutes existed, mostly in Yorkshire and Lancashire, and one of them was established at Skipton.

The premises were to serve for a time as a police station, the gaol being in a small basement room. Constable Tom Lowcock maintained law and order, with occasional help from a colleague named Whittingham. The kind-hearted Lowcock, pitying a prisoner, was known to take him to the comparative comfort of his home in Chancery Lane, where he handcuffed him to the oven door.

Angus Nicholson, a Scotsman who became sub-steward of the Skipton Estate in the 1850s, roused Skipton from its lethargy and stimulated development by pressing for the extension of the term for which leasehold land was sold from 60 to 99 years. Nicholson was commended in an article that appeared in the *Craven Herald*, stating that 'it was chiefly owing to his efforts also that the traditional unwillingness to sell freehold property was thus overcome'. His efforts made it possible for two major housing developments, at Newtown and Middletown.

The mid-19th century, with the much-resented newspaper tax abolished, was boom time for the printed word. In early times newspapers were newspapers in name only, being virtually devoid of news and advertisements, but containing flowery statements that amounted to little more than polite begging. The first local newspaper, the *Skipton Advertiser and Monthly Recorder* (proprietor John Garnett), commenced publication in December 1852. In the following year the first issue of the *Craven Herald*, launched by a printer named Robert Tasker as a monthly mouthpiece for Conservatism, appeared with a circulation of about 700 copies.

A writer in the *Craven Weekly Pioneer and General Advertiser* eulogised about the Penny Readings at the Mechanics' Library, a cultural diversion that began in 1862. Extracts from prose and poetry were interspersed with music and singing. 'These entertainments will in some measure be found inducing the working men of the town to prefer the amusements that appeal to their better nature and elevate their moral and social condition, rather than the extravagant and debasing satisfaction of sensuality in the licensed pest-house.' The sight was 'beautiful', the hall illuminated by 'the sunshine of happy human faces'.

Profound changes to the fabric of Holy Trinity Church followed a natural disaster. On 19 June 1853, during a thunderstorm, lightning struck the building during a service and the aisle was spattered with stones that had fallen from the roof. A stove pipe collapsed, dusting the congregation with soot. The repair of the church cost £1,470, of which £620 was donated by the patron, Christ Church, Oxford. In the restoration, a concrete floor was laid, sealing in the burial vaults and graves. A report into the sanitary conditions, quoted in *Skipton 2000*, noted:

> In most instances, the only partition between the living and the dead is a single slab of stone and a few inches of earth. These offered but a very imperfect barrier to the escape of noxious effluvia and slowly therefore, but incessantly, the gaseous products of decomposition were effused into the atmosphere of the church. But at the night services, established in 1843 when gas was introduced into the church, when the air became rarefied by the warmth of stoves and burning gas, the rank vapours were drawn out in uncontrollable profusion. It is impossible to say what mischief was done by this and how many, while worshipping within the sanctuary, have breathed the atmosphere of corruption and have sickened unto death.

Catholics worshipping in the private chapel of the Tempests of Broughton Hall had their small numbers augmented in the 1820s when Baldisaro Porri and his family arrived. The two families combined to build a church in the town, which took form in the 1840s, with St Stephen as its patron. Numbers continued to grow, leading to the church's enlargement in the 1850s. Nonconformity prospered, too, despite periods of intolerance. George Fox, founder of the Quakers, visited Skipton in 1658. Quakerism was so despised by Thomas Sutton, a 17th-century vicar, that on 5 February 1666 he recorded in the register details relating to the death of Jonathan, the son of John Scott of Skipton, a Quaker, adding to the entry: 'Christened by I knowe not whom and buried as they pleased at Bradley.'

John Wesley preached in the town from just outside the home of John Garforth and his disciples built a place of worship on Chapel Hill in 1791; it was rebuilt in 1821 and in turn replaced by a much larger chapel in Water Street (eventually transformed into local government offices). A Primitive Methodist chapel, built at Millfield in 1835, was closed in 1880 with the opening of a larger chapel on Gargrave Road. This was one of those splendid places of worship that annually, just before Christmas, presented *Messiah* by Handel, with celebrated principals and a choir of around a hundred. The chapel was demolished in the 1970s and the site used for a block of flats.

In 1857 William Ranger investigated the sanitary condition of the town, which was without a governing body 'though it had considerable inhabitants'. In the absence of sewers, householders were inclined to divert their drainage by the handiest route into the nearest beck, but some gentlemen objected to a scheme of public sewerage. The inspector commented that 'the Criminals of our land had seven times as much space allotted to them as the poor of Skipton have'. The prisons were cleaner, sweeter and purer than some of the rented dwellings he had visited. The report had a happy consequence in the formation of a Local Board of Health (the precursor of the council).

Dr E.W. Benson, Archbishop of Canterbury, visiting relatives in Skipton in 1892, recalled boyhood memories of a once beautiful Airedale. He remembered 'its slopes and its copses and ridges and clear stream and grey stone farms and nothing other than small villages'. Now he beheld the valley 'growing into one dismal connected street with nothing to elevate a single idea. What can people do but be Radicals, who see Nature's beauty daily disappearing and man doing nothing that is not ugly and cheap. The whole valley from end to end is spoiled, enslaved, dejected. It was the very home and spring of fresh air and water, and now it is a sewer of smoke, with a mantling ditch.'

In 1862 Skipton acquired a Town Hall. It was built on the site of the Old Vicarage by the Public Buildings Company at a cost of £4,500 and impressed by its classical style, complete with columns and pediments. In 1895 the Urban District Council bought the Town Hall for an amount similar to the initial cost. At the other end of the main street was Caroline Square, named after Caroline of Brunswick, wife of her cousin, the Prince Regent, later George IV.

In late Victorian times, this was the setting for travelling menageries. The authorities spoke about 'obstruction', but the excitement and colour of such exotic events enlivened the somewhat drab lives of the majority of Skiptonians. The Square lost such delights when, in 1877, an elephant wrapped its trunk round a passer-by. Three years later, when Jane Day arrived in town with her menagerie, the *Craven Herald* commented that the Local Board did not care to have the town blockaded with vans of wild beasts, and that 'pens of the domesticated brutes on fair days are more than they can satisfactorily stomach'. The police attempted to stop Mrs Day's entry into town and she threatened to let her lions loose on them. The police allowed the show to go ahead, but six years later, when James Edmonds, owner of Wombwell's Menagerie tested the law, he was served with 20 summonses. Caroline Square was no longer considered a suitable venue for wild beasts, friendly elephants and excitable townsfolk.

The first mention of what became known as the Skipton Show occurred, ironically, in an issue of the *Settle Chronicle* for October 1855. It was revealed that 'the capital of Craven' inaugurated its Agricultural Society by a Show of Cattle, etc., on 20 September: 'Mountebanks, Red Indians, quack doctors and auctioneers vied with each other in desperate efforts to snatch a harvest from the passers-by to the superior attraction of the day.' Visitors were confronted with triumphal arches embellished with evergreens, national flags, banners and streamers in red, white and blue. In the evening 'a grand display of fireworks' was succeeded by a celebration of victories in the Crimean War, described as 'a general illumination in commemoration of the fall of Sebastopol'. In 1876 the organisers of the Skipton Show gracefully

109   *Hospital Gala Day, with a float entered by Dewhurst's Mill.*

gave way to those planning the Great Yorkshire Show, which that year took place at Bold Venture, Keighley Road, and the last of the Skipton Shows was held in 1929.

W.H. Dawson's *History of Skipton* was published in 1882. Dawson was a Skiptonian born in 1860, the son of the John Dawson who had founded a temperance newspaper, *Craven Pioneer*. In the book *Skipton 2000: The Millennium Walk*, Ian Lockwood, the present editor of the *Craven Herald & Pioneer*, consulted Dawson's diaries to find out how this comparatively young man did the research. He had his daily job at the *Pioneer* but, by rising at 5 a.m. and trawling through documents in Skipton Castle and the Petyt Library both early and late in the day, his classic history was created. In his eighties, Dawson recalled yet more of life in his native town, including polls in Skipton taken when only 414 men were eligible and the notion of a secret vote was unknown. The voter headed for the hustings, a wooden stage in full view of the street, and announced his choice of candidate. Cheers or groans greeted his words.

The 19th century was also a time of sobering up, the chapel having great support and the temperance movement a period of success culminating on Whit Monday 1872 with the opening of a large Temperance Hall. Adult education was encouraged and in 1887 there opened on a main street site, purchased from the Castle Estate for £1,500, a library, newsroom, conversation room, lecture theatre and classrooms. The year 1894 saw the opening of Skipton's first college, the Science & Art School, when the town was decorated with bunting. A band played in the High Street. The lecture theatre, stepped so steeply that it must have induced attacks of vertigo in some, was

Thon
Lind
1807-

110   *Thomas Lindley,
parson at Halton Gill
and Hubberholme,
portrayed in stained
glass at Hubberholme
Church while crossing
Horse Head Pass.*

to become the venue of the Craven Naturalists' and Scientific Association. Shops fronting High Street were removed in 1908 and two years later an imposing new frontage for the library was in place. The funds benefited from a £3,000 grant from the Carnegie Trust. Sir Nikolaus Pevsner described Skipton Library, in 1981, as 'the only building that runs counter to this modest street ... too high, two townish'.

The golden anniversary of the Queen's reign was observed in June 1887, the gentlemen of the town meeting in the yard of Brick Hall to inspect a fine ox that would be killed and roasted for the local celebrations. Ten years later, to mark the Diamond Jubilee, lime trees were planted beside High Street. When local people met to decide how the Jubilee should be marked, Lord Hothfield of Skipton Castle headed a list of subscribers for a cottage hospital, in preference to a public library, which was built where Granville Street joined Brook Street. Victoria died in 1901. Since her reign had begun, Skipton had lost its insularity, being linked to the canal and rail systems of the land.

Skipton Rural District Council, covering 228 square miles, first met in the Board Room of the old Skipton Guardians on a cheerless day in December 1894. R.R. Waterhouse, who wrote a short history of the council (1894-1974), mentioned that one or two members, who had probably risen early and done four or five hours work on a farm before setting out for Skipton, tended to doze off as they sat in the Board Room, whereupon the chairman, John Arthur Slingsby, who was severely crippled and walked with the aid of two sticks, would bring one of them down on his desk with terrific force. This almost caused the slumbering one to jump out of his skin. An Urban District Council was formed under the Local Government Act of 1895.

In the 19th century, with busy weekly cattle markets, Skipton had become the economic centre of much of Craven and a major producer of dairy products for the industrial towns immediately to the south. Linked by canal, rail and road with the west, the town replaced its woollen industry with one based on cotton and a dominant sound was the clatter from rows of Lancashire-type looms.

Chapter 12

Craven's Heritage

Culture in the Craven Dales has combined that of the native-born with the vast and varied contribution made by visiting writers, artists and musicians, many of whom settled in the area. The derogatory term for the last-named was 'off-comer' or 'offcumden'. With the population of true dalesfolk declining, and the 'off-comers' gaining numerical superiority, the distinction has become blurred. Dales life evolved in isolation but the Craven Dales were not as cut off from the outer world as was a northern region such as Swaledale.

Hubberholme church, at the head of Wharfedale, is widely known for its air of antiquity and for its medieval rood-loft. Church and inn, which lies just across the bridge and was once the vicarage, are still linked by the Dales Parliament, or the Letting of the Poor Pasture, the proceeds of which benefited the poor of the parish

111 *Hubberholme church interior, featuring font and rood-loft.*

in times past. In Victorian days two local farmers wrote a song of Upper Wharfedale more notable for the names of local people than for its lyrics. An example:

Grace Pawson's the next, she keeps the George Inn,
Many a good dalesman kens th' taste of her gin.
Hard by lives the parson, he's very good,
While Edmund Dixon's snug under the wood.

The Poor Pasture is a 16-acre field on Kirkgill pasture. Customarily, a service in church precedes the letting, which at the inn begins with the ringing of a bell suspended over the bar. A candle, some three inches long, is lit, placed in a saucer and set on a windowsill. The vicar and his associates occupied one of two rooms, known for the evening as the 'House of Lords', hence the Dales Parliament.

Nonconformity regenerated dale country life, first through the Quakers and later, especially, the Methodists, whose hymn book was 'the Bible set to music'. John Wesley had visited the area and so, in June 1750, did a great friend, the Rev. George Whitefield. Having addressed crowds in the West Riding and Lancashire towns, he retired to the house of Giles Batty, his old and much-respected friend who lived at Newby Cote, between Ingleton and Clapham, and wrote to his patron, the Countess of Huntingdon, reporting on progress. Just before the letter was posted he added a

footnote: 'Last night Satan shewed his teeth. Some persons got into the barn and stable and cut my chaise and one of the horses' tails. What would men do if they could?' Several friends, anticipating something of the kind, had promised to keep watch during the night. They announced themselves as 'light sleepers', but the mischief-makers were too wily for them.

A rich aspect of Craven's heritage is passing with the decline of rural Methodism, which had made a strong appeal to a plain, unpretentious people. The local preacher who occupied the pulpit on most Sundays was 'yan of us', his speech full of dialect and his sermon containing homely references, especially those to shepherds and sheep. A reminder of the early days of Methodist worship in a remote area was Mill Dam, a farmstead near Bentham, at the edge of the Craven Dale country. Worshippers gathered in the front room and sat on forms that had been stored in a barn. A rostrum was slipped over the back of a chair. When the

112 *Hubberholme church, Upper Wharfedale.*

preacher's concentration strayed he had a view, through the single window, of majestic Ingleborough.

Among the earliest of the visiting poets was William Wordsworth, a friend of the Rev. William Carr, a romantic whose family provided incumbents of Bolton Abbey for over a century up to 1843. Bolton Abbey was the setting for a fanciful tale relating to the White Doe of Rylstone. The man who introduced Wordsworth to the legend – and it was no more than that – was John Marshall, a wealthy flax-spinner of Leeds, who married a schoolfriend of Dorothy Wordsworth. The two families were on affable terms. In 1807 Marshall took Wordsworth to Bolton Priory and the woodland walks and outlined the story of

113   *The Rev. George Whitefield, friend of John Wesley, who visited Newby Cote, near Clapham.*

the White Doe, which sprang from a squabble over deer-hunting rights between the Cliffords and the Nortons, their small-time neighbours. Mary Norton had a pet deer which accompanied her to worship at Bolton and, after her death, lay on her grave during divine service. Marshall suggested that J.M.W. Turner, who was then making sketches to illustrate Whitaker's *History of Richmondshire*, might illustrate the work, but Turner declined the offer and Birkett Foster provided the illustrations.

114   *St Alkelda's Church, Giggleswick. 'Keld', which features in the saint's name, means 'spring'. The village has several notable wells.*

Local poets' efforts rarely exceeded the level of doggerel. Tom Twisleton, who farmed at Winskill, on high ground near Stainforth, was different. His *Splinters Struck Off Winskill Rock*, published in 1867, is exceptional. In the introduction he both explained and excused his use of local dialect:

> For we who speak this dialect,
> To grammar fine an' words correct
> We hev but sma' pretence;
> A' when our speeches, rough an' queer,
> Fa' on a finely-polished ear,
> 'Twill hardly sound like sense.

Arthur Raistrick observed in *The Pennine Dales* (1968): 'Art has little chance to flourish where the terms of living are hard and most livelihood is not far above a subsistence level.' It was the visiting artist rather than the writer who made the Craven Dales widely known in the later stages of what became known as the Romantic period. Thomas Girton, who became familiar with Wharfedale in 1796, portrayed the Priory ruins against a late evening sky, with light reflected in the river. It was almost certainly he who introduced Turner to the area. Turner's great friend and patron in Yorkshire was Walter Fawkes, of Farnley Hall near Otley, which Turner used as a base for part of each summer until the death of his friend in 1825. According to John Ruskin, the notable Victorian art critic, the melancholy beauty of Bolton Priory greatly influenced Turner's art.

115 *Bridge House, Arncliffe, which was visited by the author Charles Kingsley.*

MILK! MILK!! MILK!!!

SWEET SEPARATED MILK,

DIRECT FROM

LINTON FALLS CREAMERY,

WHICH IS, FOR DOMESTIC PURPOSES, EQUAL TO NEW.

A trial of the above is earnestly solicited, as the proprietors are of opinion that once tried it will be always used.

DELIVERY FROM HOUSE TO HOUSE.

N.B.—Fresh Cream, Mignon, Coulumbia, and Skim Milk Cheeses ; also Sweet Cream and Fresh Butter supplied daily <u>to Order.</u>

Edwin Henry Landseer (1802-73), Queen Victoria's favourite artist, was familiar with Bolton Priory in a passing way. Wearing a maroon velvet shooting coat, he made sketches hereabouts for a painting commissioned by the Duke of Devonshire. The painting delivered by the artist, entitled 'Bolton Abbey in Olden Time', displeased the Duke, being an interior study when an exterior one was expected. Exhibited at the Royal Academy in 1834, however, it gave the upper Wharfe valley wide publicity and attracted discerning tourists.

The Dales watercolourists of old were inclined to put away their equipment and paints in high summer, when there were just a thousand shades of green. The favourite season of Marmaduke Miller, of Arncliffe, was early spring. Reginald Smith, who illustrated Halliwell Sutcliffe's *The Striding Dales*, finding green a difficult colour to work with, preferred the sober browns and greys of winter and early spring. Smith was born and educated in Skipton, studied art at Keighley, and in 1910 was a student-in-training at the Royal College of Art in South Kensington. After a year of study in Italy, and another spell in London, Smith returned to Yorkshire in 1918, establishing a studio on a hillside overlooking Grassington. He was an early-morning artist with a preference for quiet tones, and observed, 'There's a certain tranquil beauty about the day when the sun is rising – something quietly lovely about the hills and the river when the world is half-asleep.' His life ended abruptly when he drowned in The Strid in his beloved Wharfedale. His clothes were found on rocks at one side of this turbulent stretch of river; his art materials lay on the other.

R.G. Brundrit (1883-1960), born in Liverpool, was brought to Yorkshire at the age of three and educated at Bradford Grammar School before going on to the Slade. A founder of the Wharfedale group of painters, Reggie – as he was known to family and friends – worked from a studio at Grassington, capturing Craven life and landscapes with a quick and easy technique. He was prolific yet not showy. *The Times* obituary writer was to observe: 'Few painters can have made their reputation

117   *Road repairs at Settle.*

with less sensation than Reginald Grange Brundrit.' The Royal Academy displayed over 200 of his pictures between 1906 and 1961. Some of the finest works from his early period in Craven were snow scenes. 'In the Grip of Winter' was acclaimed at the Royal Academy before being displayed overseas. His colour sense and technique were outstanding. On a day when rain flooded his paint box, he worked furiously. Back home, he was about to burn the canvas when it was rescued by his family. Brundrit's most famous portrait, 'Fresh Air Stubbs', a study of a Grassington character, is now in the Tate Gallery.

John F. Greenwood, who became best-known as a wood engraver, was born in 1885 and concluded his training at the Royal College of Art in 1911. He became a fine interpreter of the Craven Dales, his woodcuts capturing the strength and drama of the fells, the bounding vigour of the roads, the grey stone walls and the rugged simplicity of the Dales hamlets. He combined prose, illustration and his love of country places in his book, *The Dales are Mine*, published in 1952.

118   *Gledstone's Fair at Settle. The venue was the capacious market place.*

Joan Hassall, another of the country's most notable wood engravers, visited Malham in 1932 and afterwards remarked, 'It was just like falling in love; I have never been the same since.' She described the dale as 'unrelentingly noble, full of surprises and unfoldings'. Joan retired to Malham 46 years later after a career spent in London illustrating books for leading publishers. Among the works for which she provided engravings was Margaret Lane's classic biography of the Brontës. Also associated with Malham for much of her life was Constance Pearson (1886-1970), whose art training took place in Leeds. Constance developed a fondness

119   *Joan Hassall, wood engraver, spent her later years in Malham.*

for limestone scenery, invariably painting outdoors and sometimes returning home with a painting showing splash marks from rain. Her granddaughter, Katharine Holmes, has turned watercolours of the landscape into mixed media paintings using all manner of materials picked up on site.

Pen pictures of the Craven Dales include articles and essays by J.B. Priestley, who wrote an introduction to the first issue of *The Yorkshire Dalesman* in April 1939. Having been demobilised from the Army in the spring of 1919, the very first writing job he was given was 'to do some articles on a little walking tour in the Dales'. He would never forget the start of that tour in Wharfedale, and 'the sunlight that set all the dewdrops glittering about my path that morning. On many return visits, the Dales have never disappointed me.' Writing in *Life International* in 1966, he described Upper Wharfedale, one of his favourite dales, as 'a narrow grass-and-limestone valley … Its smallest place, Hubberholme – just a bridge, an inn and a church, all old – is sheer magic, not quite in this world. Lower Wharfedale, around Bolton Abbey and Barden Tower, is altogether gentler, a charm of deep woods and a sparkling river…' Priestley preferred 'sterner stuff'. His ashes were interred in the churchyard at Hubberholme, a hamlet he had described as 'one of the pleasantest places in the world'.

Halliwell Sutcliffe, novelist, had to struggle to make his way. The first of 32 novels from his pen was published in 1893. From 1907 until his death in 1932, he lived at the house he re-named White Abbey at Linton-in-Craven. He will be best remembered for *The Striding Dales*, which is an appealing blend of fact and fiction. Sutcliffe worked chiefly at night, retiring to his study about 8.30 and writing until the early hours, putting on paper all he had felt and experienced during the day, when he pottered in his garden or went for a cycle ride. He gave a chilling account of Greenhow, perched on its hill at an elevation of 1,200 feet. 'These are the wild lands, grim, silent, waiting for the true spring to come, waiting for a summer that at last will thaw their inner cold … Sheep nibble everlastingly at wiry grasses, thin as the reedy, whistling breeze…'

120   *Snow Castle, Upper Settle, 1886. This was large enough for trestles and forms to be admitted so teas might be served. (Drawing by Marie Brockbank.)*

Sutcliffe developed a legend of numerous cobblers hammering away at the hidden hamlet of Thorpe, in Wharfedale, making footwear for the monks of Fountains. Tucked away from the gaze of the world, they were not troubled by marauding Scots. The legend-busting Raistricks – Arthur and Elizabeth, who lived nearby in Linton – could find no confirmation of the link between Thorpe and Fountains Abbey. And some other villages in the locality supported more cobblers than had Thorpe.

Raistrick, a Dales historian with a prolific output, who lived into his nineties, considerable enriched our knowledge of the region and its heritage, and was dubbed 'man of the millennium' by the Yorkshire Dales Society. Arthur claimed that one of the surest ways to spiritual renewal and physical well-being was to love, cherish and explore the countryside. From 1924 until 1929 he researched in mining geology and was for almost thirty years a lecturer, then Reader in Geology, at King's College, Newcastle-upon-Tyne. A Quaker who endured imprisonment as a conscientious objector in the First World War, he retired at the start of the Second World War, taking up residence in a converted barn at Linton-in-Craven. His study, only ten feet square, had a three-light window on the south and a brick fireplace. On either side were bookshelves and cupboards. If he felt the need for privacy – or an escape from draughts – he drew a curtain across the gap. He developed through his interests and writings what became known as 'industrial archaeology'. He also had a long association with outdoor movements, especially the Ramblers' Association and the Youth Hostels Association, and was a member of the first planning committee of the Yorkshire Dales National Park (West Riding section).

Arthur Conan Doyle, creator of Sherlock Holmes, had family links with Masongill, a tucked-away hamlet in North Craven where his mother resided for twenty years. He was married to Louise Hawkins at Thornton-in-Lonsdale church, near Ingleton, in 1885. The Jesuits at Stoneyhurst had educated him but his wife was a Protestant whom he met at Southsea, when Arthur was a newly qualified doctor treating her brother. The Doyles lived in Edinburgh, where Charles, Mary's husband and Arthur's father, was an artist, an alcoholic and an epileptic who in 1883 or 1884 was committed to a mental hospital in Dumfries. A cash-strapped Mary took in as lodger one Bryan Waller, a lecturer at Edinburgh University. Waller inherited the Masongill estate, moved to the big house and installed Mary Doyle (and her last child) in a nearby cottage, where she resided until May 1917.

Arthur Conan Doyle knew Masongill as 'this little moorside village'. His visits to his mother were spasmodic, but he wrote her over 1,500 letters and respectfully called her 'the Ma'am'. A believer in fairies, he suspected that some must live in the potholes on the fell beyond the hamlet. He played golf at Park Foot, a working farm in Ingleton where a course had been contrived. Rumours that Waller's relationship with Mary was more than platonic cannot now be substantiated. She was a conspicuous figure, dressing herself in dark clothes, wearing a bonnet and using for transport a wickerwork dog cart with a pony in the shafts. She died in 1921. Happily married to Jean Leckie, his second wife, Arthur Conan Doyle became one of the best known and most handsomely rewarded writers of his generation. He spent most of his life in the south, but there is more than a hint of the north in some of his splendid books. He died after a heart attack at his Sussex home in July 1930.

121   *Marriage certificate of Arthur Conan Doyle, issued at Thornton-in-Lonsdale, near Ingleton.*

122 *Cecil Slingsby, climber and writer, took long holidays from the family mill at Carleton, near Skipton.*

William Cecil Slingsby, born at Carleton near Skipton in 1849, was a prominent member of the Yorkshire Ramblers, whose delight was to climb crags and descend potholes; they were among the first to exploit the Craven Dales as a playground. Slingsby became an author through his interest in mountaineering. As a young man, his imagination was set alight by reading of the stirring deeds in alpine areas of the world recounted by Edward Whymper. It was in Norway, a country little known to British visitors, that he felt most at home. By popularising that land, he helped the Norwegians achieve a better living, so that it was popularly said the country had two patron saints, St Olaf and Cecil Slingsby. While here he realised that much sport might be obtained from skis, which had been a mode of transport in Norway for centuries, and he introduced Norwegian-type skis to the Alps.

123 *Austwick School, typical of many village schools throughout Craven.*

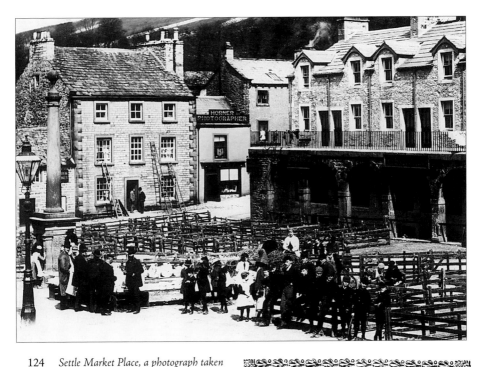

124   *Settle Market Place, a photograph taken by Dr Buck, medical practitioner and friend of the composer Edward Elgar. Buck had his surgery at the large building on the left.*

125   *Mr Garstang's account, issued in 1835, for what seems to have been a convivial evening.*

Settle played a part in the career of Alf Wight, the veterinary surgeon whose books featuring James Herriot became best sellers and were dramatised in a series of television productions. Donald Sinclair, who employed Wight at Thirsk, had moved here from Settle, where in the early 1930s he was an adviser to the Ministry of Agriculture and concerned with such down-to-earth matters as sheep scab. Donald was handsome, dashing and charming – and the owner of a big Lagonda car. At Thirsk, in 1939, when business was brisk, he gave the newly qualified Alf Wight his first job. In his books, Wight immortalised Donald as the irascible Siegfried Farnon.

R. GARSTANG,

The Hart's Head,

GIGGLESWICK.

	£	s	d
EATING, &c.			
Tea and Coffee			
Rum, Brandy and Gin	,,	11	0
Punch, Wine and Negus			
Ale, Porter and Tobacco	,,	,,	6
Cyder and Fruit			
Paper and Postage			
Washing			
Servants' Eating and Ale			
Horses' Hay and Corn			
Beds and Chamber Fire			
Beasts, Sheep, &c.			
Waiter and Chambermaid			
Ostler and Boots			
Blacksmith and Saddler			

£ 11 6

(*WALKER, SETTLE.*)

126   *Notable cricket victory for Settle. In the rear is a viaduct of the Settle-Carlisle Railway.*

127   *Settle Conservative Club billiards team, winners of the League Cup, 1902.*

Leta Douglas's contribution to Craven's heritage was in recording local folk dances in the 1930s, when there were still old folk who remembered and might demonstrate them. Leta, who lived at Giggleswick, raised one, then two folk-dancing teams in the Settle area and organised annual tours of the Craven Dales. She chatted with old folk, recording the melodies and dance steps from the village hops of many years before. 'Meeting Six', the first local dance she studied, was shown to her during a morning playtime in one of the Upper Wharfedale schools and was still featured in dances organised at Kettlewell. Two collections of dances were published. The first, entitled *Six Dances of the Yorkshire*

128   *The composer Delius, who was especially fond of Barden Tower, in Wharfedale.*

Dales, appeared in November 1931, and ran to 13 editions, copies being sent to the United States and to exiles in lands then known as the British Empire.

No great music was composed in the Craven Dales, but popular tunes were absorbed into local concerts and dances, where musical accompaniment was by fiddle and melodeon. The strains of brass bands were to be heard on every side. Delius, born in Bradford, died in France and, having expressed a wish to be buried in an English

129   *Folk dancers in Settle Market Place. Leta Douglas recorded dances that had a local flavour.*

churchyard was, inexplicably, interred at Limpsfield, on the Surrey-Sussex border. His music, evocative of shimmering sunlight and quiet landscapes, is a blend of the idioms of Europe and North America (where he lived for a spell in Florida). A Craven connection was brought out in a *Dalesman* article written by Margaret de Vesci, daughter of Claire, his favourite sister, who noted that Delius had ridden a pony across Ilkley Moor and swum in the Wharfe. He loved the grandeur of the dale country and the characteristic folk who inhabited it. In the book *Memoirs of My Brother, Frederick Delius*, she related how he brought his just-completed score of *Koanga* for her opinion. While staying with her in Brontë Country, he and Claire rode over the moors on horseback to look at Wuthering Heights. He loved to hear or read about the Cliffords of Skipton, and at Barden Tower, in Wharfedale, he

130 *Harry Cockerill, with concertina, played at dances throughout the Craven Dales.*

131 *Richard Clapham and family, Austwick Hall.*

132 *Annie Clapham (right) with her Swedish governess.*

133 *A Victorian interior. Austwick Hall, home of the Clapham family.*

was fascinated by the Shepherd Lord's interest in astrology. Delius revisited Yorkshire periodically during the First World War, and during his last debilitating illness he was fond of recalling his Yorkshire boyhood, and in particular the stone setts in a Bradford street, steam trams, cricket, and the hardy folk of the Craven Dales.

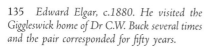

134   *Dr Charles William Buck, friend of Edward Elgar.*

135   *Edward Elgar, c.1880. He visited the Giggleswick home of Dr C.W. Buck several times and the pair corresponded for fifty years.*

136   *Malham Tarn, 1857. The 150-acre estate lies at an elevation of over 1,200 feet.*

Dr Charles William Buck, of Giggleswick, was introduced to Edward Elgar, then a young musician and conductor, at the centenary celebrations of the British Medical Association in Worcester in 1882. Elgar persuaded Buck, via a mutual friend, to bring along his 'cello and take his place in an orchestra that was being mustered for a late-evening soirée. While chatting afterwards, the two young men found a common interest in animals, the countryside and music. The result was that Buck invited Elgar to visit him at Giggleswick. He did so, by train, changing at Leeds.

Elgar had several short holidays at Giggleswick and Settle in the 1880s. The two men were fond of light-hearted japes, such as kidnapping Miss Buck's parrot and bearing it – the cage on a pole supported by the two men – into Settle. As they were crossing Settle Bridge, the bottom of the cage fell out and a bemused

137   *Walter Morrison, the 'Craven millionaire', who referred to Malham Tarn House as 'my mountain home'.*

parrot was dumped on the ground. During the day, they walked and talked. A letter written by Elgar to Buck's daughter, Monica, was illustrated, sparsely, using several quickly drawn lines, with an impression of a cat – 'one of the cats your father and I hunted on the scars'.

A bundle of scores composed by Elgar and signed by him as from 'Giggleswyke', a favourite term for the village, were given to me by the lady to whom they had been bequeathed and were subsequently donated to the Elgar Foundation. In the collection was the harmonisation of 'Clapham Town End', a local dialect song that Buck jotted down on hearing it rendered in a local inn. The silly theme involved two horse-dealers discussing the sale of horses they owned: the horse belonging to the seller was dying; the horse owned by the other was dead, but after the transaction the purchaser was richer by 'a hide and fower [four] shoes'. Elgar did not care to work on music written by others, yet to satisfy the longing of an old friend he did the harmonisation, based on Buck's recorded melody. He signed the work and dated it 15 September 1885. Here is the first verse of a composition, the meaning of which must have bemused Elgar:

> Bane to Claapham own-gate lived an oud Yorkshire tyke,
> Who i' dealing i' horseflesh hed ne'er met his like;
> 'Twor is pride that i' aw the hard bargains he'd hit,
> He'd bit a girt monny, but nivver bin bit.

138 *A Victorian boating scene, Malham Tarn, when the estate was owned by Walter Morrison. The Tarn was noted for its fine trout.*

At the present day, Arthur Butterworth, who lives at Embsay near Skipton, has developed many musical themes while walking on the Yorkshire moors. As a conductor, including years conducting the Settle Orchestra, Arthur has a particular predilection for Elgar, directing many performances of his music. Living in the Craven Dales, he composed *The Quiet Tarn*, an orchestral piece inspired by what he refers to as 'the glorious 1st June, 1959, and a first visit to Malham Tarn'. *A Dales Suite* was written in 1964 for the band of Ermysted's Grammar School at Skipton.

139 *John Whittingale Winskill, agent at Malham Tarn, who enjoyed being mistaken for the owner.*

140 *In the Stable Yard at Malham Tarn House. Morrison, who loved the outdoors, preferred to walk rather than ride.*

Sir William Milner, architect and garden designer, worked artistically in stone and slate. Though he was a York man, between 1927 and 1960 he became a familiar figure in Skipton and Craven. Indeed, it was not easy to overlook him, for he stood 6ft 7in tall and was broadly built. Sir William visited Wharfedale to find a place where he might live. His choice was Parcevall Hall, a 17th-century longhouse on a virtually treeless hillside near Appletreewick. The building had a clear view across a small valley to Simon Seat, a prominent moor-edge feature. Parcevall Hall was sensitively restored and extended, earth and rock removed from behind the building being laid before it in the form of terracing. A splendid garden was added. Sir William's special interest in alpine plants led to his prominent association with the Northern Horticultural Society, who were developing a trial ground at Harlow Car, Harrogate.

Chapter 13

Recent History

Local government reorganisation in 1974 did away, at least for administrative purposes, with the ancient Ridings of Yorkshire. Skipton and most of historic Craven, which had been in the West Riding, now repose in North Yorkshire – a vast county extending across the Pennines to the coast. There were administrative hiccoughs at Skipton, where new arrangement meant that the library and museum had to be run separately. Craven District Council assumed control of the museum, with its host of exhibits donated freely by many people. A professional staff now run what is a treasure house of Craven history and traditions on the first floor of the Town Hall annexe.

When I was young, the approach to Skipton from the south was through a pastoral landscape with a backdrop of hill until, suddenly, the road dipped and was flanked by neat rows of houses and the occasional mill. Today, with the town by-passed, the inevitable in-filling has taken place. The motorist negotiates a roundabout at Snaygill and then travels through an industrial area, complete with traffic lights and a variety of white road markings. The by-passes do at least keep most of the traffic from what was once the High Street bottleneck, but the street remains busy. Nearly

141 *Austwick village shop in the days of Mrs Harrison Hodgson.*

142 *Gala Day at Skipton. The procession musters before moving through the town.*

seventy years ago, when it was less so, a crowd of youngsters following an old custom assembled on the road beside grocers' shops on New Year's Day. They cheered, then scrambled for money or goods.

There are by-passes elsewhere in Craven. One stretch of new road, wide and straight enough to accommodate aircraft, directs traffic from the main street of the large village of Addingham. Extremely tall buildings, constructed here in the handloom days, once gave the feel of a rock gorge. Settle is by-passed, athough, with no handy, direct way to the A65, many quarry vehicles drive right through the town. Clapham's by-pass took a swathe of good land and the new road has wide grassy verges that, in spring, provide rest and grazing for the horses of the travelling folk *en route* for Appleby Fair. The road to Malham has been improved only on the final, straight, downhill stretch to the old village. The chapel was once the first building to be seen; now there is an information centre and car park.

The High Street at Skipton looks pretty much as it ever did: a broad street, 'twixt the church and Caroline Square, with an imposing war memorial (recently renovated and cleaned), a Town Hall with a classical façade (and a red telephone box on either side of the entrance) and a separate block of buildings forming the Middle Row. A Skiptonian returning after a long absence would notice many new firms, some with garish shop-fronts.

Gone are Waterfalls bookshop, with its minstrels' gallery, and Stockdale & Helm the grocers. The Manby family relinquished their ironmonger's shop, which now has other uses, although a clock set in the gable end remains. This was one of the first clocks in the land to be illuminated but it ceased ticking some years ago. Gone

143   *Wilfred Procter, first warden of the Yorkshire Dales National Park.*

144   *National Park warden in the Craven Dales. Wardens are now called Rangers.*

145   *Walkers at Kettlewell, from which Upper Wharfedale village footpaths radiate.*

is Robert Fell and Sons, who dealt in lead, some of it from the workings on Grassington Moor. Their products were sheet lead, water pipes and gas tubing, but, when trade for such items declined, they turned first to related products then closed in 1998.

Ermysted's Grammar School, founded by Peter Toller over 500 years ago, is a voluntary aided school with over 600 pupils. Ermysted's and Skipton Girls' High School are two of the best state schools and it is partly because of their reputation that a host of families have moved into the catchment area, making Skipton one of the wealthier places in the land. Craven College, a relative newcomer, provides education for over 2,000 young people. The College and Skipton Building Society may both be traced back to the witness of philanthropic people in the 19th-century town. The Building Society is by far the largest local employer of labour, its extensive new buildings beside the Bailey the workplace of a thousand people, with thousands more based in other centres. As the town adjusted itself to shopping and tourism, Smith's Yard became the stately Craven Court in 1957, and today is a stylish covered shopping centre.

Bolton Abbey, where a few Augustinian canons prayed and ministered, is now the centrepiece of an extensive estate and remains one of the most popular and enchanting tourist attractions in the Craven Dales, with over half a million visitors a year. The £5 charge for car parking helps to ensure the estate is self-sustaining and generates enough income for maintenance and reinvestment. On the estate are no fewer than 55 listed buildings, 87 redundant barns, a glorious reach of the Wharfe, fringed for most of the way by woodland and grouse-haunted moors, and 85 miles of public and permissive paths.

The Rev. A.P. Howes, a former Rector of Bolton Abbey, wrote a 'complete guide' to the Abbey and Woods in 1904 which foresaw the evolution of a new country-going society. Visitors might pass through the grounds and view the ruins but were urged not to leave 'paper, litter or orange peel'. Strictly prohibited were picnics, games, bands of music or bathing in the river. The Woods were out of bounds to bicycles, tricycles and vehicles containing more than eight persons. To the aforementioned litter was added 'straw and empty bottles, &c.'.

Life in the upper dales was transformed in the 1950s by the introduction of an electrical supply. When, in 1955, Litton and the surrounding villages went 'on the grid', there was a formal switching on of coloured bulbs in holly trees at Croft Guest

House by the Chairman of Settle Rural Council. The chairman of the Yorkshire Electricity Board announced the completion of an electrification scheme for the whole of Upper Wharfedale, connecting 26 hamlets. The Board had expended £3 million and set up 50,000 poles to bring electricity to remote rural areas.

The *Craven Herald & Pioneer* commented that the switch-on meant that paraffin lamps were being thrown away and the centuries-old tradition of milking by hand would die out as farmers switched to machines. In Wood Lane, Grassington, a new

146   *Features of Bolton Abbey, a tourist 'honeypot', by the River Wharfe.*

147   *Modern transport. A young farmer with his 'quad', the term for an all-terrain vehicle. When 'kenning' sheep, his dog rides pillion.*

148   *Start of one of the first Three Peaks Races, a springtime event. A cyclo-cross involving the Peaks takes place in autumn.*

149   *Ribblehead Viaduct, on the Settle-Carlisle Railway. The 24-arch structure carries a regular passenger service and many goods trains.*

stone-built telephone exchange came into operation. Telephone users in the area could now dial directly to anywhere in the Skipton district. The new system replaced one by which callers, using the facilities of a manual exchange installed in 1907, had to call up an operator to connect them.

Much of Craven lies within the Yorkshire Dales National Park where, in addition to established footpaths, there are mapped areas on which, under the Countryside and Rights of Way (CROW) Act of 2000, one might sensibly enjoy the right to roam. The Park Authority has introduced a chain of mountain bike-friendly inns, one of which is the *New Inn* at Appletreewick. Since 1995 the inn has had a repair workshop and overnight facilities for cyclists.

150 *Ramblers heading towards the 'nose end' of Pen-y-ghent.*

Tourism has become a valuable money-earner for Skipton and the dale country. In town, boats and barges in the canal basin exist for pleasure and not for industry. In the Craven villages, the native population is declining and the number of what used to be known as off-comers has risen greatly, as has the number of small businesses catering for visitors. Tourists admire Craven's architectural splendours, including large churches at Skipton, Kirkby Malham and Giggleswick, built in the good times of the late 15th and early 16th centuries and restored with care and pride.

Walkers and cyclists follow green roads, and mountain bikers, walkers and horse riders will, by 2008, be able to traverse the Dales National Park section of a Pennine Bridleway National Trail – a section extending for 52 miles from Long Preston in the south to Hell Gill Bridge on the border between Yorkshire and Cumbria. A vast area of little-known landscape may now be roamed across as of right, and the spirit of the old packhorse and peddler days enjoyed by sensitive souls traversing such ancient footpaths as the Craven Old Way, which crosses the lunar-like Scales Moor on its way from Ingleton to Dent.

It is easy to slip away from Skipton's busy High Street via steps at the side of Mill Bridge and walk on the towpath between Eller Beck and Springs Canal. To the right is the dark bulk of the Castle Rock, still evoking times long ago when a Norman lord chose it as the site of his castle and gave Skipton a sense of importance it has never lost.

Bibliography

Barringer, J.C., *The Yorkshire Dales* (1982)

Bonser, K.J., *The Drovers* (1970)

Brayshaw, Thomas and Robinson, Ralph M., *A History of the Ancient Parish of Giggleswick* (1932)

Brigg, John J., *The King's Highway in Craven* (1927)

Bruff, Harald John Lexhow, *Character Sketches of Old Yorkshire Lead Miners* (undated)

Butlin, Robin A. (ed.), *Historical Atlas of North Yorkshire* (2003)

Carter, Stephanie and Weatherhead, Alexandra, *Craven College: A History of Further Education in Skipton* (1999)

Dalesman, The, various issues

Dawson, W.H., *History of Skipton* (1882)

Dickinson, J.M., *Mines and t'Miners* (1972)

Eyres, Patrick, 'The Building Works of Lady Anne Clifford', *New Arcadians' Journal* No. 17 (1985)

Gibbon, A.M., *The Ancient Free Grammar School of Skipton in Craven* (1947)

Goodhart, J.S., *Lead Mining* (1985)

Harker, Bailey J., *Upper Wharfedale* (1869)

Hartley, Marie and Ingilby, Joan, *The Yorkshire Dales* (1956)

Hey, David, *Yorkshire from A.D. 1000* (1986)

Holmes, Martin, *Proud Northern Lady – Lady Anne Clifford, 1590-1676* (1975)

Hudson, Rita and Philip, *Skipton: A Photographic History* (2001)

Hurtley, Thomas, *A Concise Account of some Natural Curiosities in the Envrions of Malham in Craven, Yorkshire* (1786); *Hurtley's Poems on the Natural Curiosities of Malham, in Craven, Yorkshire*, introduced by Thos Brayshaw (1917)

Hutton, John, *A Tour to the Caves – in the environs of Ingleborough and Settle* (1780)

Kershaw, I., *Bolton Priory. The economy of a Northern Monastery 1286-1325* (1973)

Lingard, Philip, *First Bus in Yorkshire* (1975)

Lockwood, Ian (compiler), *Skipton 2000 – The Millennium Walk* (1999)

Mitchell, W.R., *Elgar in the Yorkshire Dales* (1987); *Mr Elgar and Dr Buck: a Musical*

Friendship (1991); *Music of the Yorkshire Dales* (1997); *Edward Elgar in the Yorkshire Dales* (1999); *The Story of the Yorkshire Dales* (1999)

Morrison, John, *Lead Mining in the Yorkshire Dales* (1998)

Pontefract, Ella and Hartley, Marie, *Wharfedale* (1938)

Raistrick, Arthur, *Grassington and Upper Wharfedale* (1948); *The Pennine Dales* (1968); *Lead Mining in the Yorkshire Dales* (1972, 1981); *Mines & Miners on Malham Moor* (1983); *Arthur Raistrick's Yorkshire Dales* (1991)

Raistrick, A. and S.E., *Skipton: A Study in Site Value* (1930)

Rowley, R. Geoffrey, *Old Skipton* (1969); *The Book of Skipton* (1983)

Simmons, I.G., *Yorkshire Dales – National Park Guide No. 9* (1971)

Skipton-in-Craven Civic Society, *Historic Maps and Views of Skipton* (2003)

Speight, Harry, *Tramps and Drives in the Craven Highlands* (1895)

Spence, Richard T., *Skipton Castle and its Builders* (2002)

Sutcliffe, Halliwell, *The Striding Dales* (1929)

Thomson, J. Radford, *Guide to the District of Craven* (second edition, 1879)

Waltham, Tony, *Yorkshire Dales National Park* (1987)

Waterhouse, R.R., *Skipton Rural District Council (1894-1974)*

Watkins, Peter, *Bolton Priory and its Church* (1989)

White, Robert, *Yorkshire Dales* (1997)

Index

Page numbers in **bold** refer to illustrations